Maths Skills

for A Level

Economics

Jim Lawrence

OXFORD

UNIVERSITY PRESS

Great Clarendon Street, Oxford, OX2 6DP, United Kingdom

Oxford University Press is a department of the University of Oxford.
It furthers the University's objective of excellence in research, scholarship, and
education by publishing worldwide. Oxford is a registered trade mark of Oxford
University Press in the UK and in certain other countries

British Library Cataloguing in Publication Data
Data available

978-1-4085-2708-5

1 3 5 7 9 10 8 6 4 2

Printed in China

Acknowledgements
We are grateful for permission to reprint extracts from the following copyright
material:

Bar chart of UK current account adapted from data from the Office for National
Statistics licensed under the Open Government Licence v.2.0; Graph of
unemployment rates © Eurostat; Table of UK current account, exports, imports
and balance of payments sourced from the Office for National Statistics licensed
under the Open Government Licence v.2.0; Table of figures for UK capital
account sourced from the Office for National Statistics licensed under the Open
Government Licence v.2.0.

Although we have made every effort to trace and contact all copyright holders
before publication this has not been possible in all cases. If notified, the publisher
will rectify any errors or omissions at the earliest opportunity.

Links to third party websites are provided by Oxford in good faith and for
information only. Oxford disclaims any responsibility for the materials contained
in any third party website referenced in this work.

Contents

How to use this book   5

Microeconomics   6

Reading and interpreting graphical information   6
Numerous independent variables   8
Calculating areas and values   10
Representing statistical data   12
Scatter diagrams and time series data   14
Taxes and subsidies 1   16
Taxes and subsidies 2   18
Elasticity of demand   20
Cross elasticity of demand (XPEOD)   22
Income elasticity of demand (YEOD)   24
Price elasticity of supply (PEOS)   26
Returns in the short run   28
Short-run costs   30
Long-run costs   32
The meaning of profit 1   34
The meaning of profit 2   36
Perfect competition   38
The level of profit or loss   40
Monopoly 1   42
Monopoly 2   44
Imperfect competition 1   46
Imperfect competition 2   48
The labour market   50
The elasticity of supply of labour   52
Wage determination 1   54
Wage determination 2   56
Increasing labour productivity 1   58
Increasing labour productivity 2   60

Macroeconomics   62

Gross domestic product   62
Nominal and real GDP   64
Consumption, saving and expenditure   66
Price index 1   68
Price index 2   70
The Keynesian multiplier 1   72
The Keynesian multiplier 2   74
Investment 1   76
Investment 2   78

International economics   80

Absolute and comparative advantage and the terms of trade   80
Exchange rates   82
Formulae for demand and supply   84
Purchasing power parity (PPP)   86
Relative PPP   88
The exchange rate index   90
Terms of trade (TOT)   92
The balance of payments   94

How to use this book

This workbook has been written to support the development of key mathematics skills required to achieve success in your A Level Science course. It has been devised and written by teachers and the practice questions included reflect the **exam-tested content** for AQA, OCR and Cambridge syllabi.

The workbook is structured into sections with each section having a clear scientific topic. Then, each spread covers a mathematical skill or skills that you may need to practise. Each spreads offers the following features:

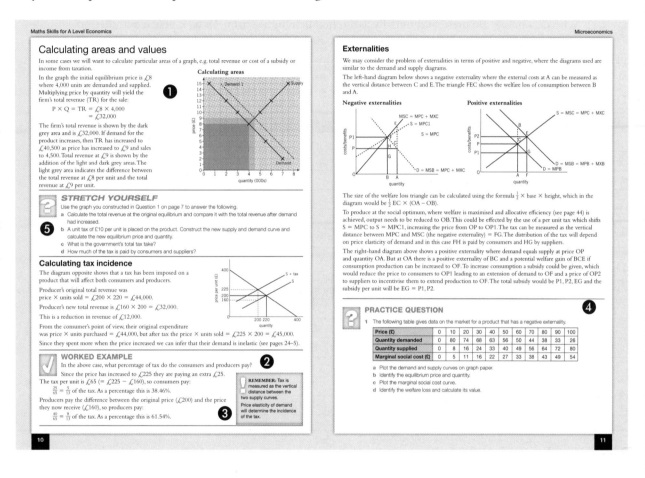

❶ *Main text* outlines the mathematical skill or skills covered within the spread.

❷ *Worked example* – each spread will have one or two worked examples to demonstrate calculations and working-out methods.

❸ *Remember* is a useful box that will offer you tips, hints and other snippets of useful information.

❹ *Practice questions* are to increase your confidence with contextual examples. Answers are available at: www.oxfordsecondary.co.uk

❺ *Stretch yourself* – some of the spreads may also contain a few more difficult questions at the end to stretch your mathematical knowledge and understanding.

Reading and interpreting graphical information

Demand and supply

During your study of economics you will come across numerous graphs and diagrams and this chapter aims to assist you in your understanding and interpretation of these. Data is extremely important in the formulation of economic theories and can be presented in a number of ways, so it is important for both understanding and examination success that you can interpret it.

✓ **WORKED EXAMPLE**

The data below are presented initially as a schedule ranging from 15 to 2 pence and then in the form of a table. It shows how the quantity demanded and supplied varies for different prices. So, for example, at a price of 15 pence demand is 500 units and supply is 7,500 units, while at 2 pence the quantity demanded is 7,000 units and supply is 1,000 units.

Demand and supply schedules

Price (pence)	Quantity demanded (units)
15	500
12	2,000
10	3,000
8	4,000
5	5,500
2	7,000

Price (pence)	Quantity supplied (units)
15	7,500
12	6,000
10	5,000
8	4,000
5	2,500
2	1,000

Demand and supply table

Price (pence)	Quantity demanded (units)	Quantity supplied (units)
15	500	7,500
12	2,000	6,000
10	3,000	5,000
8	4,000	4,000
5	5,500	2,500
2	7,000	1,000

This type of data is more often presented in graphical form, so that it can be manipulated to show how the **variables** of price and quantity are related to each other.

Constructing a graph

In a graph the vertical line (*y*-axis) begins at zero (the origin) at the bottom and the values increase as we move up the axis. The horizontal line (*x*-axis) also starts at zero and increases as we move to the right along the axis. Both axes show the units of the variable that is to be measured.

To construct a graph of the data above we scale the price values on the *y*-axis from zero, the origin, to 15 pence in ascending order up the axis. Quantity is shown here on the *x*-axis. It ranges from 500 to 8,000 units and is also scaled from zero.

The quantity demanded can then be plotted against the price. A negative relationship results, i.e. as the price increases the quantity demanded falls.

The quantity supplied, however, shows a positive relationship to price, i.e. as the price increases, the supply increases.

The graph shows a causal relationship between the two variables of price and quantity demanded and supplied as a change in the price will cause both the quantity demanded and supplied to change.

The variable that causes the change is called the **independent variable** while the variable that is affected as a result of the change is called the **dependent variable**.

The amount that consumers demand and that suppliers are prepared to supply depends on the level of price so both quantity demanded and supplied are dependent variables while price is the independent variable.

Conventionally in mathematics the dependent variable is plotted on the y-axis and the independent variable on the x-axis. This practice is followed in economics except in the case of demand and supply diagrams that reverse the usual mathematical convention by plotting the independent variable on the y-axis and the dependent variable on the x-axis.

Demand and supply curve

(Graph: price (pence) on y-axis from 0 to 15, quantity (000s) on x-axis from 0 to 8, showing a Supply curve rising from (1,2) to (7.5,15) and a Demand curve falling from (0.5,15) to (7.5,2), intersecting at (4,8). Broken lines at price 12 to quantity 2 and 6.)

Analysing the graph

While plotting graphs may be relatively straightforward, reading and interpreting graphs is of great importance. For example, at a price of 12p the quantity demanded is 2,000 units, but 6,000 units are supplied, so from an economist's point of view there is excess supply, which will initiate changes in the behaviour of suppliers. The excess supply can be calculated by placing a straight edge horizontally across the graph at 12p, which allows the required supply and demand figures to be read off by going vertically downwards to the quantity on the x-axis, as shown by the broken lines in the diagram.

Similarly at a price of 5p the quantity demanded (5,500 units) exceeds the quantity supplied (2,500 units) and there is pressure on price to increase.

At both AS and A2 Level in Economics we tend to use diagrams similar to that above to portray information. The basic difference between the diagram and the graph is that the graph is more precise and accurate than the diagram, but for purposes of analysis the diagram is usually sufficient for our requirements. Most of the diagrams that you will construct are unlikely to contain figures but you must be able to appreciate the position of the curves and what they mean.

PRACTICE QUESTION

1 The table contains information regarding the demand and supply of a certain commodity.
   a Plot the demand and supply curves on graph paper.
   b What is the equilibrium price and quantity?
   c Assuming that demand increases by 10 units at all prices, what are the new equilibrium price and quantity?

Price (£)	Quantity demanded (units)	Quantity supplied (units)
10	50	0
20	45	0
30	41	14
40	37	27
50	32	41
60	28	55
70	23	69
80	19	83

Numerous independent variables

In reality both demand and supply (the dependent variables) are dependent on more than just price (the independent variable) because demand and supply are likely to depend on factors other than price.

To deal with such a large number of variables we plot the relationship between price and quantity on the basis of 'all other things being equal', which means that apart from the relationship under consideration all other factors remain constant. To illustrate how independent variables will affect supply or demand we shift the demand or supply curve to illustrate whether the quantities have increased or decreased.

This is shown in the diagram opposite where the demand curve has shifted to the right, showing an increase in the quantity demanded of the product at all prices.

Independent variables

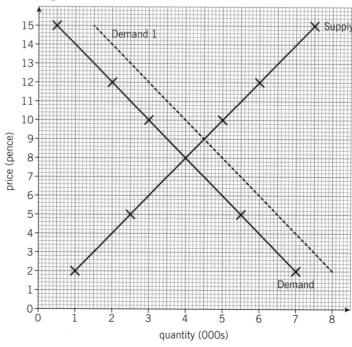

PRACTICE QUESTION

1 **a** List the independent variables that can affect
   i demand   **ii** supply.
   b Construct diagrams to show the effect of these independent variables on supply and demand.

Maximum and minimum relationships

Some graphical relationships in economics have a maximum or a minimum.

WORKED EXAMPLE

The left-hand diagram on the following page shows the relationship between profit and quantity produced, and has been produced from the following table.

The relationship is one that starts with a positive slope and reaches a maximum at which its slope is zero, and then moves into a range in which its slope is negative.

Output (000s)	Profit (£000s)
0	0
10	20
20	39
30	54
40	64
50	66
60	90
70	41
80	21
90	0

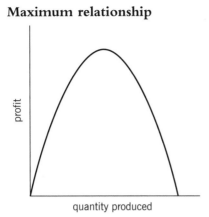

Maximum relationship

profit

quantity produced

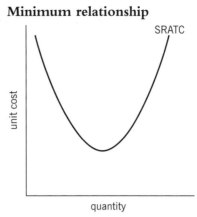

Minimum relationship

SRATC

unit cost

quantity

The right-hand diagram shows a minimum point. The relationship begins with a negative slope, falls to a minimum and then becomes positive. The example shown is a short-run average total cost curve where costs initially fall, reach their lowest point and then begin to increase as diminishing returns set in. This relationship starts out with a negative slope, reaches a minimum at which it is zero, then moves into a range where the slope is positive.

Graphs with positive and negative relationships

Unless positive and negative relationships are linear, in which case they will be graphed as straight lines, they will be curves which may become more or less steep as shown by the diagrams below.

Figures 1 and 4 show a linear relationship whose slope is constant.

Figures 2 and 5 show a positive/negative relationship whose slope becomes steeper as we move horizontally away from the origin – a positive/negative relationship with an increasing slope.

Figures 3 and 6 show a positive/negative relationship with a slope that becomes less steep as we move away from the origin.

Figure 1: linear

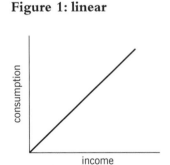

consumption

income

Figure 2: positive becoming steeper

price level

positive becoming steeper

real output

Figure 3: positive becoming less steep

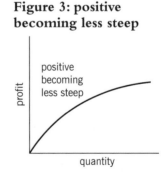

profit

positive becoming less steep

quantity

Figure 4: linear

price

negative linear

quantity

Figure 5: negative becoming steeper

capital goods

negative becoming steeper

consumer goods

Figure 6: negative becoming less steep

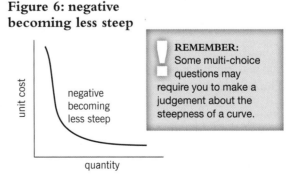

unit cost

negative becoming less steep

quantity

> **REMEMBER:**
> Some multi-choice questions may require you to make a judgement about the steepness of a curve.

Calculating areas and values

In some cases we will want to calculate particular areas of a graph, e.g. total revenue or cost of a subsidy or income from taxation.

In the graph the initial equilibrium price is £8 where 4,000 units are demanded and supplied. Multiplying price by quantity will yield the firm's total revenue (TR) for the sale:

$$P \times Q = TR = £8 \times 4,000$$
$$= £32,000$$

The firm's total revenue is shown by the dark grey area and is £32,000. If demand for the product increases, then TR has increased to £40,500 as price has increased to £9 and sales to 4,500. Total revenue at £9 is shown by the addition of the light and dark grey areas. The light grey area indicates the difference between the total revenue at £8 per unit and the total revenue at £9 per unit.

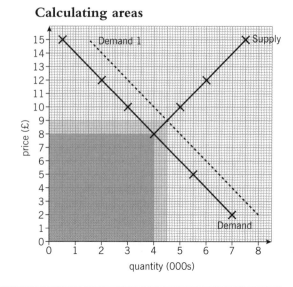

Calculating areas

STRETCH YOURSELF

Use the graph you constructed in Question 1 on page 7 to answer the following.

a Calculate the total revenue at the original equilibrium and compare it with the total revenue after demand had increased.

b A unit tax of £10 per unit is placed on the product. Construct the new supply and demand curve and calculate the new equilibrium price and quantity.

c What is the government's total tax take?

d How much of the tax is paid by consumers and suppliers?

Calculating tax incidence

The diagram opposite shows that a tax has been imposed on a product that will affect both consumers and producers.

Producer's original total revenue was
price × units sold = £200 × 220 = £44,000.

Producer's new total revenue is £160 × 200 = £32,000.

This is a reduction in revenue of £12,000.

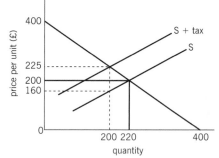

From the consumer's point of view, their original expenditure was price × units purchased = £44,000, but after tax the price × units sold = £225 × 200 = £45,000.

Since they spent more when the price increased we can infer that their demand is inelastic (see pages 24–5).

WORKED EXAMPLE

In the above case, what percentage of tax do the consumers and producers pay?

Since the price has increased to £225 they are paying an extra £25. The tax per unit is £65 (= £225 − £160), so consumers pay:

$\frac{25}{65} = \frac{5}{13}$ of the tax. As a percentage this is 38.46%.

Producers pay the difference between the original price (£200) and the price they now receive (£160), so producers pay:

$\frac{40}{65} = \frac{8}{13}$ of the tax. As a percentage this is 61.54%.

> **REMEMBER:** Tax is measured as the vertical distance between the two supply curves.
>
> Price elasticity of demand will determine the incidence of the tax.

Externalities

We may consider the problem of externalities in terms of positive and negative, where the diagrams used are similar to the demand and supply diagrams.

The left-hand diagram below shows a negative externality where the external costs at A can be measured as the vertical distance between C and E. The triangle FEC shows the welfare loss of consumption between B and A.

Negative externalities

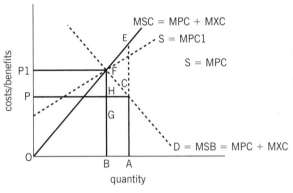

Positive externalities

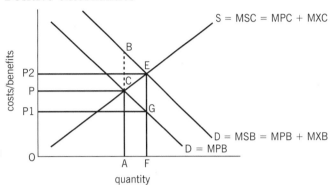

The size of the welfare loss triangle can be calculated using the formula $\frac{1}{2} \times$ base $\times$ height, which in the diagram would be $\frac{1}{2}$ EC $\times$ (OA − OB).

To produce at the social optimum, where welfare is maximised and allocative efficiency (see page 44) is achieved, output needs to be reduced to OB. This could be effected by the use of a per unit tax which shifts S = MPC to S = MPC1, increasing the price from OP to OP1. The tax can be measured as the vertical distance between MPC and MSC (the negative externality) = FG. The distribution of the tax will depend on price elasticity of demand and in this case FH is paid by consumers and HG by suppliers.

The right-hand diagram above shows a positive externality where demand equals supply at price OP and quantity OA. But at OA there is a positive externality of BC and a potential welfare gain of BCE if consumption production can be increased to OF. To increase consumption a subsidy could be given, which would reduce the price to consumers to OP1 leading to an extension of demand to OF and a price of OP2 to suppliers to incentivise them to extend production to OF. The total subsidy would be P1, P2, EG and the subsidy per unit will be EG = P1, P2.

PRACTICE QUESTION

1 The following table gives data on the market for a product that has a negative externality.

Price (£)	0	10	20	30	40	50	60	70	80	90	100
Quantity demanded	0	80	74	68	63	56	50	44	38	33	26
Quantity supplied	0	8	16	24	33	40	49	56	64	72	80
Marginal social cost (£)	0	5	11	16	22	27	33	38	43	49	54

a Plot the demand and supply curves on graph paper.

b Identify the equilibrium price and quantity.

c Plot the marginal social cost curve.

d Identify the welfare loss and calculate its value.

Representing statistical data

Pie charts

These are a very effective way of showing the relative sizes of economic data.

 WORKED EXAMPLE

The table shows the market share of the UK supermarket industry.

When this information is displayed in a pie chart it is clear how the whole market is divided between the various supermarkets. Construction of the chart is relatively simple:

As there are 360 degrees in a full turn, each percentage point of the market represents $360° \div 100$, so each percentage point is represented by an angle of $3.6°$. For example:

Tesco's market share, in degrees, is $26.0 \times 3.6 = 93.6°$. Using a protractor and a ruler it is possible to construct pie charts quite accurately.

Market share of UK supermarkets

Supermarket name	Supermarket share (%)
Tesco	26.0
Asda	13.2
Sainsbury's	12.5
Morrisons	9.1
Somerfield	3.5
Marks and Spencer	3.5
Waitrose	3.1
Co-op	2.6
Others	26.5

Pie chart of market share of UK supermarkets

Shares of UK food and grocery retailing 2006

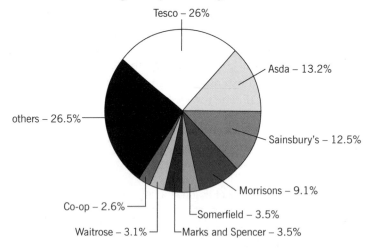

The pie chart makes more of a visual impact, and we can see that Tesco has the largest market share. You are likely to come across pie charts when studying oligopoly in order to calculate the concentration ratio. This is the percentage of market share held by, say, the three largest firms, which in this case would be Tesco, Asda and Sainsbury's with a total market share of $26.0 + 13.2 + 12.5 = 51.7\%$ of the total market.

Pie charts are limited in that they only present one set of data and do not always allow for easy comparison of information, and for this reason pie charts are used mainly as above.

PRACTICE QUESTION

1 **a** Calculate the three- and five-firm concentration ratios.
   b What do these ratios tell you about the organisation of the industry?
   c How could further concentration occur?

> **REMEMBER:** When calculating, for example, the three-firm concentration ratio, add the percentages for the three firms with the largest percentages.
>
> Do not include 'others' in your calculations as 'others' refers to smaller firms.

Market concentration in the bus industry

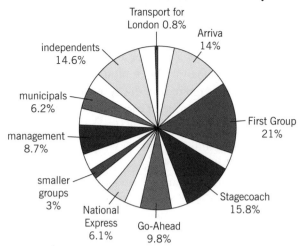

Transport for London 0.8%
Arriva 14%
independents 14.6%
municipals 6.2%
management 8.7%
smaller groups 3%
National Express 6.1%
Go-Ahead 9.8%
Stagecoach 15.8%
First Group 21%

Bar charts

The same information about supermarkets is presented right in the form of a bar chart or graph with percentage of the market on the vertical axis and the supermarket on the horizontal axis.

Bar charts provide a visual interpretation of size that cannot easily be seen in pie charts. They illustrate cross–section data with the figures taken for a single variable at a point in time. The bar chart provides a visual representation showing that, for example, Tesco had a market share of 26% while Sainsbury's had a 12.5% market share.

Bar charts can also show negative values. The figure below shows the UK current account for 2008 to 2012 with negative values throughout.

Bar chart of market share of UK supermarkets

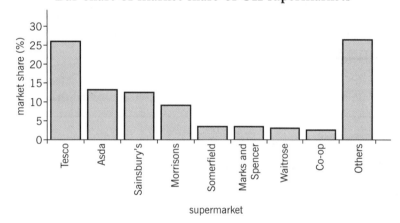

> **REMEMBER:** Check the position of the zero carefully before interpreting data.

Negative bar chart showing the UK current account

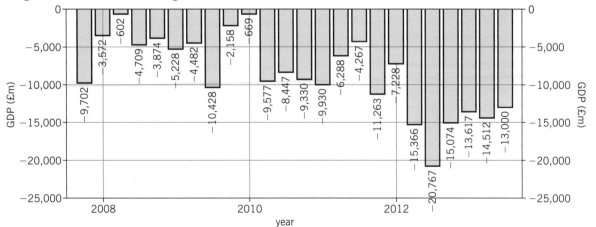

Source: www.tradingeconomics.com; UK Office for National Statistics

Scatter diagrams and time series data

Scatter diagrams

A scatter diagram is a tool for analysing relationships between two variables. One variable is plotted on the horizontal axis and the other is plotted on the vertical axis. The diagram on the right plots the price of cars against their age, and indicates that as cars age their prices fall. The pattern of points shows the relationship graphically and we can say that there is a **strong correlation** in the data.

Correlation shows that two sets of data are linked together: positive when the values increase together and negative when one value increases as the other decreases.

Correlations are useful because they can indicate a predictive relationship that can be exploited in practice. While the diagram in the above case shows a correlation between two variables, it does not by itself prove that one variable causes the other. There may be other factors at work, and there are examples where the prices of cars actually increase as they age. The dots in this scatter diagram form a pattern, which suggests there may be a causal relationship, but other scatter diagrams often indicate that variables are not closely related. This is called **weak correlation**.

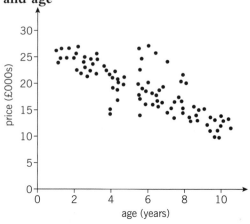

Scatter diagram comparing car price and age

Time series data

These are used to show how a variable changes over an extended period. Graphs such as these are common in data response questions at AS and A2 and it is essential that you know how to interpret them.

 ### WORKED EXAMPLE

The graph below shows unemployment rates in the EU–28, EA–17, US and Japan, seasonally adjusted, for January 2000 to September 2013. It covers a period of 13 years and allows us to make comparisons between individual countries.

It can be seen that there is a trend of unemployment rates rising in all areas except Japan, where the rates have slightly decreased from 4.755 to 3.9%.

As well as identifying trends you should comment on the highest or lowest points. Here the rapidity of change for the US in particular could also be mentioned.

Unemployment rates in the EU–28, EA–17, US and Japan

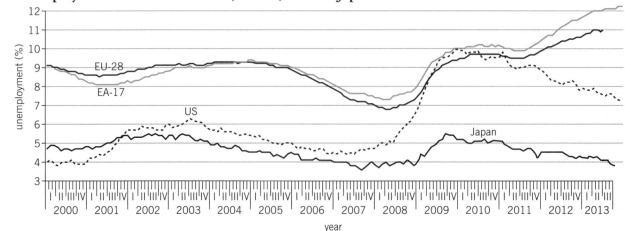

Source: Eurostat

Graphs with two axes

Variation in the price and world stocks of wheat from 2004 to 2011

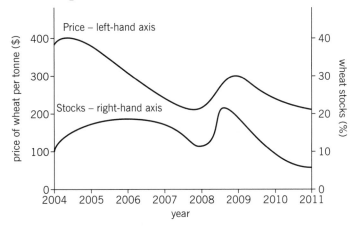

The diagram above shows a situation in which two variables are related to each other. Care must be taken with interpretation to ensure that the data are related to the correct axis. This can probably be best accomplished by using a ruler to measure against the opposite scale. For example, at the start of 2006 stocks had grown to about 18% while price per tonne was about $300.

Various factors could be noted, e.g. that the rate of both price and stocks fell over the period as a whole, or that price peaked in mid–2004 while stocks were at their highest mid–way between 2008 and 2009.

PRACTICE QUESTION

1 Using the diagram above identify two significant points of comparison between changes in the world price of wheat and the quantity of wheat stocks over the period shown.

Taxes and subsidies 1

The diagram below right has been constructed for an initial equilibrium of £5 where 30 units are demanded and supplied. It has been constructed on the basis of the following equations:

Equilibrium where $Qd = Qs$, or for market clearing $Qd - Qs = 0$.

$$Qd = a - bP$$
$$Qs = c + dP$$

The linear demand function is $Qd = a - bP$ where

Qd = quantity demanded
    (the dependent variable)
  P = price (the independent variable)
  a = the quantity intercept
  b = the slope = $\dfrac{\Delta Qd}{\Delta P}$

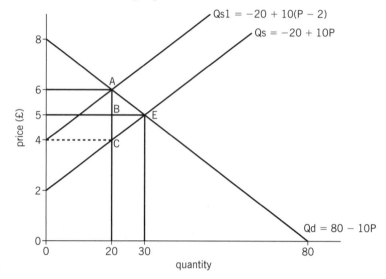

$Qs1 = -20 + 10(P - 2)$
$Qs = -20 + 10P$
$Qd = 80 - 10P$

WORKED EXAMPLE

From the data above, the demand curve is given by:

$$Qd = 80 - 10P$$

By setting P at different values the quantity demanded at each price can be determined.

Start with the Q intercept and assume that $P = 0$.

Then $Qd = 80 - 10(0) = 80$, so we can assume that at zero price 80 will be demanded.

At, say, $P = 7$, $Qd = 80 - 10(7) = 80 - 70 = 10$.

As the demand curve is linear, it can be plotted just by joining the two points for £0 and £7.

The linear supply function is $Qs = c + dP$ where

Qs = the quantity supplied (the dependent variable)
  P = price (the independent variable)
  c = the quantity intercept
  d = the slope = $\dfrac{\Delta Qs}{\Delta P}$

WORKED EXAMPLE

From the data above, the supply curve is given by:

$$Qs = -20 + 10P$$

Using zero is not very helpful as it will produce negative 20 – not a very likely supply quantity – so assume $P = 3$.

$$Qs = -20 + 10(3) = -20 + 30 = 10 \text{ at a price of £3.}$$

Now put $P = 7$:

$$Qs = -20 + 10(7) = -20 + 70 = 50 \text{ at a price of £7.}$$

As previously, join the points for £3 and £7 to produce a linear curve.

WORKED EXAMPLE

The equilibrium quantity is where demand equals supply so in the previous case,

$$Qd = 80 - 10P = Qs = -20 + 10P$$

Thus $80 - 10P = -20 + 10P$

Adding 10P to each side of the equation,

$$80 = -20 + 20P$$

Now adding 20 to each side,

$$100 = 20P$$

So $P = 5$

Substituting $P = 5$ into the demand equation gives:

$$Qd = 80 - 10(5) = 80 - 50 = 30.$$

Alternatively, substituting $P = 5$ into the supply equation gives:

$$Qs = -20 + 10(5) = -20 + 50 = 30 \text{ as before.}$$

Thus the equilibrium occurs at £5, where demand and supply are equal at 30 units.

As price × quantity sold = £5 × 30 units = £150, the supplier receives £150 for the sale of the product.

Suppose the government decides to impose a tax of £2 per unit. This can be shown on the diagram as a new supply curve drawn £2 vertically above the original one. This is because the amount supplied will be reduced at every price by the amount of the tax as it will increase the supplier's costs of production.

Alternatively we could modify the formula to take the tax into account:

The new supply formula becomes $Qs = c + d(P - T)$ where T equals the tax.

 WORKED EXAMPLE

Applying the new formula to the above case, the formula will be:

$$Qs = -20 + 10(P - 2)$$

So at £8 the quantity supplied will be:

$$Qs = -20 + 10(8 - 2) = -20 + 10(6) = -20 + 60 = 40$$

At £5, $Qs = -20 + 10(5 - 2) = -20 + 30 = 10$

Joining the quantities at £8 and £5 will produce the new supply curve Qs1.

There are a number of outcomes of the imposition of the tax in the above example:

• Quantity demanded and supplied has fallen from 30 to 20 units.
• Price to consumers has increased from £5 to £6, so consumption expenditure has fallen from £150 to £120 (price × quantity demanded = £6 × 20 = £120).
• Supplier's revenue has fallen as suppliers now receive £4 per unit = £4 × 20 units = £80.
• The tax is shown by the vertical distance AC, which is between £4 and £6, so government income increases as it receives £40 in tax (£2 tax per unit on 20 units).
• The tax is shared equally between suppliers and demanders as both pay £20. AB of the tax from £5 to £6 is paid by consumers while BC of the tax from £4 to £5 is paid by suppliers.
• Employment in the industry is likely to fall as production has decreased from 30 to 20 units.

Taxes and subsidies 2

The incidence of the tax

To determine the incidence of the tax the following formula is used:

$$\frac{\%\ \text{of tax incidence on consumers}}{\%\ \text{of tax incidence on producers}} = \frac{PES}{PED}$$

where

$$PED = \frac{\%\Delta Qd}{\%\Delta P}$$

WORKED EXAMPLE

Continuing with the case on page 17,

$$\%\Delta Qd = \frac{30 - 20}{30} = \frac{10}{30} = 0.33$$

$$\%\Delta P = \frac{6 - 5}{5} = \frac{1}{5} = 0.2$$

$$PED = \frac{0.33}{0.2} = 1.65$$

So PED is elastic.

As the percentage change in quantity and price is the same for both PED and PES, the figure will be the same for both. Thus $\frac{PES}{PED} = 1$, indicating that they both pay the same proportion of tax.

The social surplus

The original social surplus was made up of the consumer and producer surplus.

Referring to the diagram on page 16, the original consumer surplus before tax was bounded by the triangle 5, 8, E, and working on the area of a triangle as $\frac{1}{2}$ × base × height then $15 \times 3 = £45$ is the consumer surplus. (The horizontal line 5 to E is 30 when measured on the base; the height is from 5 to 8.)

The new consumer surplus after tax is $\frac{1}{2}$ × base 20 (6 to A) × height 2 (6 to 8) = **£20**. Consumer surplus has fallen by £25.

The original producer surplus was the triangle bounded by 2, 5, E which is (5 to E) $\frac{1}{2}$ base 30 × 3 (2 to 5) = £45.

The new producer surplus is $\frac{1}{2}$ × base 20 (4 to C) × height (2 to 4) = **£20**. Producer surplus has fallen by £25.

Government surplus is the rectangle 20 (0 to 20) × 2 (4 to 6) = **£40**.

Social surplus = producer surplus + consumer surplus + government surplus
$$= £20 + £20 + £40 = £80.$$

The previous surplus was consumer surplus (£45) + producer surplus (£45) = £90.

The social surplus is less than it was previously because of the welfare loss triangle AEC, which can be calculated using $\frac{1}{2}$ × base × height = $1 \left(\frac{1}{2} \text{ of 4 to 6}\right) \times 10$ (20 to 30) = £10.

Because of the tax the economy has suffered a welfare loss of £10. Do remember, however, that if this good had negative externalities the economy may have benefitted by its reduced production and consumption.

Subsidies

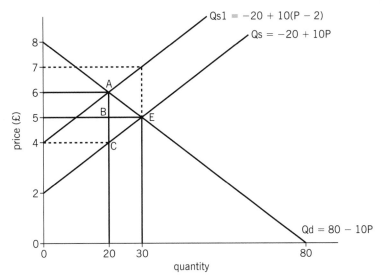

Using the information above and reproducing the original diagram, suppose that the initial equilibrium is at £6, where 20 units are demanded and supplied. If the good/service has positive externalities then they may wish to subsidise it in order to increase its production and consumption.

In order to increase consumption to 30 units the price to consumers will have to be reduced to £5, while to increase production to 30 units the price will have to increase to £7.

Effect of a subsidy

 WORKED EXAMPLE

In the above case, suppose a subsidy reduces the price to consumers from £6 to £5.

Consumer expenditure changes from £120 (price £6 × Qd 20) to £150
(price £5 × Qd 30) so we can assume that demand is elastic.

Producer's income increases from £120 price (£6 × Qd 20) to £210 (price £7 × Qd 30).

Increase in quantity demanded and supplied is from 20 to 30 units.

There is a likely increase in demand for workers.

There is a reduction in costs for firms that use the subsidised good or service.

 PRACTICE QUESTION

1 a i Construct a diagram where the demand curve is given by Qd = 60 − 5P and the supply curve is given by Qs = −15 + 10P.
Price ranges from zero to £10 and quantity varies from zero to 80.
  ii What are the equilibrium price and quantity?
  iii Calculate the firm's total revenue.
  b Assume that as a result of a government subsidy the supply curve shifts and is given by Qs = −3 + 10P.
   i Plot the curve.
   ii What are the new equilibrium price and quantity?
   iii Plot and calculate the total subsidy.
   iv Calculate the firm's new total revenue.

Elasticity of demand

Percentages

Percentages allow us to make easy comparisons of otherwise difficult figures. For example, it isn't obvious whether 35 parts out of 86 or, shown as a fraction, $\frac{35}{86}$, is greater or smaller than, say, 60 parts out of 140, or $\frac{60}{140}$.

To make the comparisons easier to see, we can convert the fractions to percentages.

 WORKED EXAMPLE

To convert $\frac{35}{86}$ into a percentage the numerator (35) is divided by the denominator (86) and the answer multiplied by 100, so

$$35 \div 86 = 0.406976744\ldots = 0.407 \text{ (to 3 significant figures)}$$
$$0.407 \times 100 = 40.7\%$$

To reverse the process, i.e. change a percentage to a fraction, divide the percentage by 100 and then simplify the fraction.

 WORKED EXAMPLE

75% as a fraction is $75 \div 100$ or $\frac{75}{100} = \frac{3}{4}$

To change a percentage into a decimal, divide the percentage by 100, which we can do just by moving the decimal point two places to the left.

 WORKED EXAMPLE

78% becomes $78 \div 100 = 0.78$

Percentage changes

In economics we often have to measure the extent to which quantities change in terms of percentages. To calculate percentage change we need an initial number and a final number. The formula is:

$$\text{Percentage change} = \frac{\text{final number} - \text{initial number}}{\text{initial number}} \times 100$$

 WORKED EXAMPLE

Assume a final value of 80 and an initial value of 50. The percentage change is:

$$\text{Percentage change} = \frac{80 - 50}{50} \times 100 = \frac{30}{50} \times 100 = 60\%$$

The percentage increase or decrease will be shown by whether the answer is positive or negative.

WORKED EXAMPLE

Find the percentage change in quantity demanded for a product changed from 82 in 2010 to 63 in 2011.

$$\text{Percentage change} = \frac{63 - 82}{82} \times 100 = \frac{-19}{82} \times 100 = -23.2\%$$

The negative sign means this was a decrease of 23.2%. You might like to consider the further implications for profit, employment, etc.

We are likely to need these techniques in the calculation of **price elasticity of demand (PEOD)**, as economists measure PEOD – the responsiveness of quantity demanded to a change in price – using the formula:

$$\text{Price elasticity of demand (PEOD)} = \frac{\text{percentage change in quantity demanded}}{\text{percentage change in price}}$$

Note that all values for PEOD will be preceded by a minus sign as an increase in price leads to a fall in quantity demanded while a fall in price leads to an increase in the quantity demanded, because price and quantity demanded are inversely related. It is conventional to leave the minus sign out when quoting values.

 WORKED EXAMPLES

If a 10% increase in the price leads to a 20% fall in the quantity demanded, then PEOD is equal to 20 ÷ 10 = 2.

If a 10% fall in price leads to a 5% increase in quantity demanded, then PEOD is equal to 0.5.

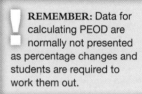 **REMEMBER:** Data for calculating PEOD are normally not presented as percentage changes and students are required to work them out.

As PEOD is measured by dividing the percentage change in quantity by the percentage change in price, another way of expressing this and working out elasticity is:

$$\text{Price elasticity of demand} = \frac{\text{original price} \times \text{change in quantity}}{\text{original quantity} \times \text{change in price}}$$

 WORKED EXAMPLE

Assume that 80 units are demanded at a price of £5 and an increase in price to £6 leads to a fall in demand to 50 units. Calculate the PEOD.

Method 1

To calculate the percentage change:

$$\frac{\text{final value} - \text{initial value}}{\text{initial value}} \times 100 = \frac{50 - 80}{80} \times 100 = \frac{-30}{80} \times 100$$
$$= \mathbf{37.5\%}$$

To calculate the price change:

$$\frac{\text{final value} - \text{initial value}}{\text{initial value}} \times 100 = \frac{6 - 5}{5} \times 100 = \frac{1}{5} \times 100$$
$$= \mathbf{20\%}$$

PEOD = 37.5 ÷ 20 = 1.875

Method 2

$$\text{PEOD} = \frac{\text{original price} \times \text{change in quantity}}{\text{original quantity} \times \text{change in price}} = \frac{5 \times 30}{80 \times 1} = \frac{150}{80} = 1.875$$

Cross elasticity of demand (XPEOD)

This situation occurs where a change in the price of one good will affect the demand for another good. This occurs in the case of **substitutes** and **complements**. It is equal to:

$$\text{XPEOD} = \frac{\text{percentage change in quantity demanded of good A}}{\text{percentage change in price of good B}}$$

Substitutes

WORKED EXAMPLE

A café increases the price of a latte from £1.20 to £1.80 per cup and finds that the sale of cappuccinos increase from 1,000 cups to 1,250 cups per week.

Use the expression

$$\frac{\text{percentage change in quantity demanded of cappuccinos}}{\text{percentage change in the price of lattes}}$$

and the previous technique to work out the percentage changes.

$$\frac{\text{new price of latte} - \text{original price of latte}}{\text{original price of latte}} = \frac{1.80 - 1.20}{1.20} = \frac{0.60}{1.20}$$

$$= 0.50$$

$$0.50 \times 100 = 50\%$$

$$\frac{\text{new quantity of cappuccinos} - \text{original quantity of cappuccinos}}{\text{original quantity of cappuccinos}} = \frac{1,250 - 1,000}{1,000} = \frac{250}{1,000}$$

$$= 0.25$$

$$0.25 \times 100 = 25\%$$

$$\frac{\% \text{ change in Qd of cappuccino}}{\% \text{ change in P of latte}} = \frac{+25\%}{+50\%} = 0.5$$

So cross PEOD equals +0.5.

A large number for cross PEOD indicates a strong substitute relationship while a small number illustrates a weak relationship between the two substitutes.

PRACTICE QUESTION

1 The price of the Ford Fiesta increases from £10,231 to £10,840 and the sales of the Vauxhall Corsa increase from 3,250 to 3,730. Calculate the cross elasticity of demand (XPEOD).

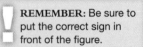

REMEMBER: Be sure to put the correct sign in front of the figure.

Complements

 WORKED EXAMPLE

The following table provides data on the price of replacement razor blades and the volume of aftershave sold.

	Price of razor blades per unit	Quantity of aftershave
January 2013	£2.20	70,000
March 2013	£2.50	64,000

Calculating the percentage change in the price of razor blades:

$$\% \text{ change in the price of razor blades} = \frac{\text{new price} - \text{original price}}{\text{original price}} \times 100$$

$$= \frac{2.50 - 2.20}{2.20} \times 100 = \frac{0.3}{2.20} \times 100$$

$$= 0.136 \times 100 = +13.64\%$$

$$\% \text{ change in the quantity of aftershave} = \frac{\text{new quantity} - \text{original quantity}}{\text{original quantity}} \times 100$$

$$= \frac{64,000 - 70,000}{70,000} \times 100$$

$$= -0.0857 \times 100 = -8.57\%$$

Substituting these values into the XPEOD formula:

$$\text{XPEOD} = \frac{\% \text{ change in Qd of aftershave}}{\% \text{ change in P of razor blades}} = \frac{-8.57\%}{+13.64\%}$$

$$= -0.63$$

The two goods are complements, so if there is a 10% increase in the price of razor blades we would expect a 6.3% fall in the sales of aftershave.

 PRACTICE QUESTION

2 Ryanair's economists have estimated the XPEOD between Ryanair flights and easyJet prices, and for Ryanair's prices and sales of its on-board perfume. However, the manager who has to use the figures does not understand them. The figures are +0.62 and −0.03 respectively. With the aid of worked examples, explain to the manager the relevance of the two figures.

Income elasticity of demand (YEOD)

This is given by:

$$\text{YEOD} = \frac{\text{percentage change in quantity demanded}}{\text{percentage change in income}} = \frac{\%\Delta Q}{\%\Delta Y}$$

There are three possibilities for income elasticity of demand:

- As income rises or falls the demand for the good rises or falls: positive income elasticity of demand – a normal good.
- A rise or fall in income has no effect on demand: zero income elasticity.
- A rise in income leads to a fall in demand while a fall in income leads to an increase in demand: negative income elasticity – an inferior good.

Positive income elasticity

WORKED EXAMPLE

	Income (£)	Number of new cars purchased
January 2013	25,500	250
December 2013	27,300	280

$$\% \text{ change in income} = \frac{27{,}300 - 25{,}500}{25{,}500} \times 100 = \frac{1{,}800}{25{,}500} \times 100 = 0.0706 \times 100$$
$$= +7\%$$

$$\% \text{ change in quantity} = \frac{280 - 250}{250} \times 100 = \frac{30}{250} \times 100 = 0.12 \times 100$$
$$= +12\%$$

The percentage change in quantity demanded is greater than the percentage change in income.

Substituting into the formula,

$$\frac{\% \text{ change in Qd}}{\% \text{ change in income}} = \frac{+12\%}{+7\%} = +1.7$$

A value for income elasticity of demand greater than 1 means that the quantity demanded is rising by a greater percentage than income. Economists refer to this situation as **income elastic**.

In the above example, should the figure have been positive but less than 1, it would have been termed **income inelastic**.

WORKED EXAMPLE

Suppose that with a 7% growth in income the quantity of cars demanded had only increased by 5%.

Then $\frac{5}{7} = 0.71$

This positive figure would signify that demand had increased but not as much as income had risen and is thus income inelastic.

Zero income elasticity

WORKED EXAMPLE

The following statement was made by a dairy farmer:

'What I can't understand is when I read that average incomes have increased from £22,700 to £24,500 why my sales of milk have not risen but remain stuck at 20,000 litres per week.'

$$\% \text{ change in income} = \frac{24,500 - 22,700}{22,700} \times 100$$

$$= +7.9\%$$

$$\% \text{ change in quantity} = \frac{20,000 - 20,000}{20,000} \times 100$$

$$= 0\%$$

$$\text{Income elasticity of demand} = \frac{0\%}{+7.9\%} = 0$$

The 7.9% increase in income has no effect on the quantity demanded and we must assume that at their current levels of income consumers can afford to consume the milk that they require. The data may have been different if consumers had a lower level of income, as the product may still have had positive income elasticity.

Negative income elasticity – inferior goods

WORKED EXAMPLE

The following data have been collected during the recession:

	Average income (£)	Sales of value baked beans
2008	25,360	88,562
2012	22,180	105,331

$$\% \text{ change in income} = \frac{22,180 - 25,360}{25,360} \times 100 = \frac{-3,180}{25,360} \times 100$$

$$= -12.5\% \text{ (a fall in income)}$$

$$\% \text{ change in quantity} = \frac{105,331 - 88,562}{88,562} \times 100 = \frac{16,769}{88,562} \times 100$$

$$= +18.93\%$$

Substituting into the formula,

$$\frac{\% \text{ change in Qd}}{\% \text{ change in income}} = \frac{+18.93\%}{-12.5\%} = -1.51$$

Thus the baked beans are an inferior good because the decrease in income has led to an increase in the quantity demanded.

The figure tells us that a 10% fall in income will lead to an increase in the quantity demanded of baked beans by $-1.51 \times -10 = 15.1\%$, while a 10% increase in income would lead to a fall of the same magnitude in the demand for the baked beans.

PRACTICE QUESTION

1 The following values are estimates of YEOD in the UK.
   a Which goods are inferior?
   b If income increases by 10% explain what would happen to
     i the sale of petrol   ii the sale of cars.
   c Explain the likely effects on bus use of a fall in income of 12.3%.

Income elasticity for	Value of YEOD
Supermarket X	−0.3
Petrol	0.55
Cars	2.4
Bus use	−0.3

Price elasticity of supply (PEOS)

Price elasticity of supply refers to the responsiveness of supply to a change in price:

$$PEOS = \frac{\text{percentage change in quantity supplied}}{\text{percentage change in price}}$$

It shows the speed at which the producer is able to change factors of production and adjust production when price changes, and indicates the degree of mobility of factors and the flexibility of production. When the good is a primary product – something that is grown, bred or mined – supply cannot be rapidly increased, but over time output can be increased as more resources can be used to ensure production.

 WORKED EXAMPLE

In the short run any increase in the price of copper can only be met by supply from existing mines and price elasticity of supply is low at 0.3. Thus a 10% increase in the price of copper would only lead to an increased supply of 10% × 0.3 = 3%, so the supply of copper is inelastic in the short run.

Over time suppose more mines can be opened and brought into operation, and the elasticity of copper supply increases to 1.4. Then a 10% increase in the price of copper will lead to a 14% increase in supply. The supply of copper has become elastic in the long run.

The example given above represents commodity markets in general, where supply in the short term is relatively inelastic. For example, both the supply of oil and petrol are relatively inelastic in the short term. Even if the price increases it is difficult to increase oil production because there is a need to drill new wells and build pipelines. Petrol needs refining and refineries may take years to build and come on stream, and therefore, with no spare capacity, it is very hard to increase production even if the price rises sharply. Thus price elasticity of supply will often be the reason why prices rise or fall quite dramatically when there are changes in demand.

In a manufacturing industry, however, a producer can run a range of products and switch between them, so supply is more price elastic than in primary production.

Importance for business

The value of PEOS is likely to be important to a business. Suppose that the PEOS is 2. As it is greater than 1 we know that PEOS is elastic.

$$2 = \frac{\text{20\% increase in quantity supplied}}{\text{10\% increase in price}}$$

Thus a 10% increase in the price leads to a 20% increase in the supply. Supply is very responsive to price and the increased supply may cause a glut in the future, followed by a fall in price leading to a decline in revenue for the supplier.

With a value for PEOS less than 1, where supply is inelastic, supply responds by a smaller amount than price change. If PEOS is 0.2 then a 10% increase in price leads to a 2% increase in supply. Suppliers are likely to increase their revenues and consumers may search for substitutes.

Determinants of elasticity of supply

Time

For a large number of goods, even though suppliers would want to increase output to increase supply this may require a considerable amount of time. This is clearly the case in agricultural and extractive markets and may also occur where firms are waiting for new capital equipment to be delivered.

We can analyse the effect of time using Marshall's three time periods:

- **Momentary equilibrium.** In this situation supply is totally inelastic. Consider a fishing boat arriving at a dock, once the boat has unloaded there is no more fish to be had and supply is inelastic at that level of catch.
- **Short-run equilibrium.** In this time period variable factors can be changed, i.e. labour and raw materials. So in the short run the boat owners can hire another crew who take the boat out as soon as the first crew get in and the supply can respond more rapidly. The supply curve becomes more elastic.
- **Long-run equilibrium.** In this period all factors of production can be adjusted. Firms can abandon old boats and build new ones, and new firms can enter the industry.

The availability of stocks or stockpiling
Firms that hold stock of finished goods are likely to have a more elastic supply curve in the short term. For agricultural goods governments may set up buffer stock programmes so that shortages can be met out of existing stockpiles.

Switching to alternative production
Clothing manufacturers, for example, may be able to switch in to lines where prices are rising and out of those where prices are falling

How costs behave as output varies
If costs rise rapidly as output expands, then the increase in supply will quickly be choked off and this will make supply more inelastic. This can be seen in the diagram right where the market for housing is shown. The equilibrium price is OP, where OA are demanded and supplied. Assume an increase in demand to D1, which is expected to lead to a new equilibrium at price OP1 and quantity of OB. If the building firms' costs rise during building then supply will be shown as S1, reflecting the increased costs and leading to a higher than expected price at OP2 and lower quantity demanded and supplied at OC.

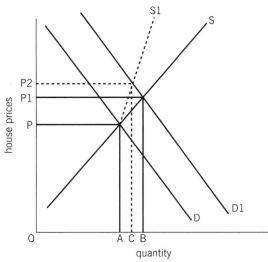

Availability of spare capacity
Firms with spare capacity have the capability to expand output relatively quickly in response to changes in the price. Firms at full capacity would find it very difficult to respond in the same way, so they would be unable to respond if prices rose.

Market contestability
If it is easy to enter a market, then resources not currently involved in the supply of a particular good may be used to enter a market when prices rise. Similarly if overseas firms see prices of a particular good rise in the UK, they may rush to enter the UK market, increasing supply.

Ability to alter production methods
If a firm can transfer to alternative methods of production such as more capital intensive production quickly, then the supply curve will become more elastic.

PRACTICE QUESTIONS

1   Explain why the short-run supply of milk in the UK may be relatively inelastic.

2   A local salon with 5 hairdressers increases its total working hours from 200 hours per week to 280 hours per week when the average price of an appointment increases from £5.50 to £7.20.
    Calculate the PEOS.

Returns in the short run

Calculation of average and marginal product

$$\text{Average product of labour (APL)} = \frac{\text{total product (Q)}}{\text{number of workers (L)}}$$

 WORKED EXAMPLE

If 5 workers produce 90 units, the average product is $\frac{90}{5} = 18$ units.

Marginal product of labour is the addition to the total product of an extra worker, i.e. extra labour unit:

$$\text{Marginal product of labour} = \frac{\text{change in total product (}\Delta\text{Q)}}{\text{change in number of workers (}\Delta\text{L)}}$$

The marginal product of labour unit 3 is the total product (TP) of labour unit 3 minus the total product of labour unit 2, or TP3 − TP2.

 WORKED EXAMPLE

The table right indicates the output of a commercial bakery that produces cakes and shows the number of workers, total, average and marginal product. Product is measured as the number of trays of cakes produced by a worker.

Number of workers	Total product	Average product	Marginal product
1	4		
2	12		
3	24		
4	42		
5	90		
6	120		
7	126		

Complete the table.

Number of workers	Total product	Average product	Marginal product
1	4	4	4
2	12	6	8
3	24	8	12
4	42	11	18
5	90	18	48
6	120	20	30
7	126	18	6

Note the following features of the completed table in the above example:
- Marginal product increases as extra workers are taken on, reducing the unit cost of making the product.
- The increased output of the extra worker (marginal product) raises the average product of all the workers, further reducing the unit cost.
- The firm has increasing marginal product until after the employment of the 5th worker, but after this point diminishing marginal returns set in, as the fixed factor becomes overloaded (perhaps there is insufficient capital equipment for the number of workers) and the falling marginal product will pull down the average product.
- Worker number 7 who only adds 6 units to production pulls down the average of all workers from 20 to 18 and as a result the average cost increases.

Average and marginal curves

The relationship between the average and marginal curves is very important in economics and is seen in a large number of diagrams. An example is shown on the right.

The marginal curve cuts the average curve at its highest point. Imagine after a number of tests your average mark was 20 but in your next test, the marginal test, your mark is 30. This higher mark will pull your average up. If your marginal mark had been 12 it would have pulled your average down. If the mark had been 20 it would have been equal to the average.

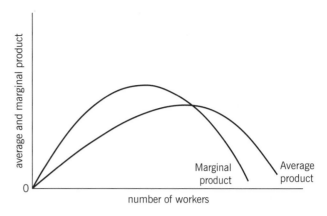

This allows us to draw certain conclusions about the relationship:
• If the marginal product is below the average then it will pull the average down and the average product will fall.
• If the marginal product is above the average then it will pull the average up.
• The marginal product will cut the average product at its highest point.

The financial value of the workers' output is known as the **revenue product** and is calculated by multiplying the workers' physical product by the price at which the cakes sell:

$$MPP \times P = MRP$$

WORKED EXAMPLE

Referring to the bakery example on page 28, if we assume that each tray of cakes sells for £10 we can work out the revenues for the firm. These are shown in the table below together with the costs.

Number of workers	Total product	Average product	Marginal product	Total revenue (£)	Average revenue (£)	Marginal revenue (£)
1	4	4	4	40	40	40
2	12	6	8	120	60	80
3	24	8	12	240	80	120
4	42	11	18	420	105	180
5	90	18	48	900	180	480
6	120	20	30	1,200	200	300
7	126	18	6	1,260	180	60

The table shows that the average revenue is maximised at 6 workers and with extra workers added average revenue falls as the average revenue of the seventh worker is £180.

The firm maximises its average revenue with 6 workers.

STRETCH YOURSELF

a Using the table below plot a graph using the information with MRP on the y-axis.
  Wage is plotted as a horizontal line with the y-intercept at the stated wage.

Number of workers	10	20	30	40	50	60	70	80	90
MRP (£ per hour)	17	30	40	48	50	48	40	30	20

b How many workers would be employed at a wage of £30 per hour?
c How many workers would be employed at £40 per hour?
d Explain why that part of the MRP curve after the 50th worker could be seen as the employer's demand curve for labour.

Short-run costs

Quantity	Fixed cost (TFC)	Variable cost (TVC)	Total cost (TC)	Average fixed cost (AFC)	Average variable cost (AVC)	Average total cost (ATC)	Marginal cost (MC)
0	550		550				
							70
1	550	70	620	550	70	620	
							65
2	550	135	685	275	68	342	
							50
3	550	185	735	183	62	245	
							40
4	550	225	775	138	56	194	
							65
5	550	290	840	110	58	168	
							90
6	550	380	930	92	63	155	
							150
7	550	530	1,080	79	76	154	
							225
8	550	755	1,305	69	94	163	

The table above indicates the total, average and marginal costs (in pounds) faced by a firm.

Diagrammatically, fixed costs appear as a straight line (see the diagram right). They are positive at zero output as the firm will incur fixed costs, e.g. a lease on premises prior to production starting. At zero output total costs must equal fixed costs.

Variable costs are zero at zero output.

> Total costs = variable costs + fixed costs
> Total costs − variable costs = fixed costs

Diagrammatically, the vertical distance between total costs and variable costs equals fixed costs.

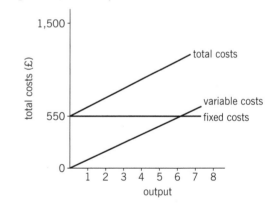

Average costs: the shape of the curves

Average total costs (ATC) are equal to average variable costs (AVC) plus average fixed costs (AFC):

> ATC = AVC + AFC

or   ATC − AVC = AFC

The curves when drawn should appear as shown:

A common mistake is to draw the AVC and ATC to be equidistant from each other throughout, whereas the distance between them will narrow as output increases.

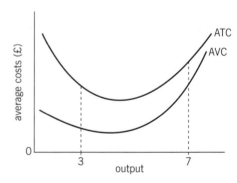

Since AFC = TFC ÷ output, as output increases the ratio decreases because a fixed number (total fixed costs) is being divided by an increasing positive number. Thus (using as an example the figures from the table above), at 3 units of output AFC will equal £183 (= £550 ÷ 3) while at 7 units of output it will fall to £79 (= £550 ÷ 7). Therefore the vertical gap between the ATC and AVC will become smaller and smaller.

WORKED EXAMPLE

Output	Fixed cost (TFC)	Variable cost (TVC)	Total cost (TC)	Average fixed cost (AFC)	Average variable cost (AVC)	Average total cost (ATC)	Marginal cost (MC)
0	750		750				
							250
1							
							230
2							
							200
3							
							280
4							
							345
5							
							400
6							
							430
7							
							500
8							

Calculate the total, average and marginal costs (all costs are in pounds).

Output	Fixed cost (TFC)	Variable cost (TVC)	Total costs (TC)	Average fixed cost (AFC)	Average variable cost (AVC)	Average total cost (ATC)	Marginal cost (MC)
0	750		750				
							250
1	750	250	1,000	750	250	1,000	
							230
2	750	480	1,230	375	240	615	
							200
3	750	680	1,430	250	227	477	
							280
4	750	960	1,710	188	240	428	
							345
5	750	1,305	2,055	150	261	411	
							400
6	750	1,705	2,455	125	284	409	
							430
7	750	2,135	2,885	107	305	412	
							500
8	750	2,635	3,385	94	329	423	

PRACTICE QUESTION

1   Use the data in the above example to work out the following:

    a Plot the average and marginal costs curves on graph paper.
        NB the MC curve must be plotted mid-way between the units of output.

    b Will the AFC curve reach zero?

    c Why does the MC fall initially and then rise?

    d At 5 units of output measure the distance between the ATC and AVC
        and the distance from the *x*-axis to the AFC – are there any similarities?

    e Will a change in fixed costs lead to a change in marginal costs?

> **!** **REMEMBER:** Do not use the word 'scale' when you are referring to the short run because it is used to describe changing all factors of production which can only occur in the long run.

Long-run costs

In the long run all factors of production are variable and the firm can change both labour and capital, so may experience increasing or decreasing returns. This can be seen in the following table.

Year	Inputs	Total product (£)	Total cost (£)	Average cost (£)
1	50	30,000	20,000	1.50
2	100	45,000	36,000	1.25
3	150	60,000	60,000	1
4	200	64,800	72,000	0.9
5	250	85,000	94,444	0.9
6	300	88,000	110,000	0.8

The firm experiences falling average costs or increasing returns to scale in years 1 to 4, constant returns to scale in years 4 and 5 and decreasing returns to scale in year 6.

Since the **long-run average total cost (LRATC)** is constructed from the lowest **short-run average total cost (SRATC)** curve for all different levels of output, we can show the relationship between short- and long-run curves and the economies of scale (see diagram right).

The short-run average total cost curves ATC1 and ATC2 both indicate a different scale of operation. At ATC2 the firm has increased its size by increasing its capital or the size of the premises. The output OQ can be produced under either situation but the lower unit cost of OB rather than OA indicates the economies of scale.

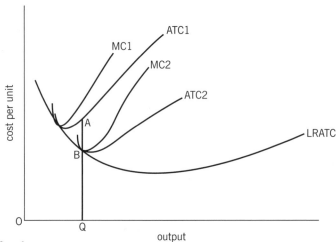

Moving between the short run and long run

Assume in the diagram right that the firm is producing 150 units of output but as a result of rising demand needs to increase its output to 250 units. The firm is unable to expand down the LRATC curve as it is in a short-run situation and the best that it can do is expand by overworking its fixed factors along the SRATC curve from A to B. If it decides to increase the quantity of fixed factors, costs will gradually fall as they come on line from B to C.

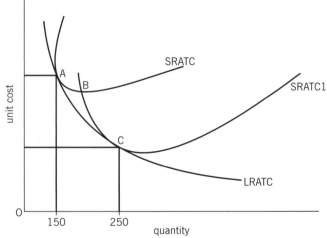

The diagram right conforms to the mathematical rule that two lines that are at a tangent have the same slope at that point so if the LRATC is decreasing then the SRATC must also be decreasing. This leads us to the conclusion that the best way to produce the output of 150 if the LRATC is falling is to build a plant in the first place where the minimum SRATC exceeds 150 at B and then underutilise it.

As most products can be produced in a number of ways, using lots of labour (labour intensive) and little capital equipment or using lots of capital (capital intensive) and a small amount of labour the producer has a choice of capital/labour combinations. The possible different ways of producing a product are known as the **consumption function** and represent a spectrum of possibilities. For example, a road may be built in India using shovels, wheelbarrows and large amounts of labour while in the USA it may be constructed using huge earthmoving equipment and a small amount of labour.

In order to decide on the composition of capital and labour the firm will take into account the marginal productivity of labour – the change in total product per unit change of labour, holding the quantity of capital constant, and the marginal product of capital – a change in total product per unit change in capital holding the amount of labour constant. Both capital and labour are subject to diminishing returns.

Substitution of capital for labour

The marginal rate of substitution of capital for labour is the decrease in capital per unit and increase in labour that keeps output constant.

WORKED EXAMPLE

The table below shows the possible combinations of capital and labour (production function) that a firm aiming to produce 20 double glazed windows per day might employ.

Production method	Capital	Labour
1	8	2
2	4	4
3	3	5

Method 1 has 8 workers and 2 units of labour whereas Method 2 has 4 units of capital and 4 units of labour.

The marginal rate of substitution of capital for labour is the ratio of the fall in capital (K) to the increase in labour (L):

Marginal rate of substitution = $\Delta K \div \Delta L = 4 \div 2 = 2$

If the firm decides to employ Method 3 then the change in capital is 1 and the change in labour is also 1 so the marginal rate of substitution is 1.

This example conforms to the law of diminishing marginal rate of substitution, which states that the marginal rate of substitution of capital for labour falls as the amount of capital decreases and the amount of labour increases.

PRACTICE QUESTION

1 A company currently has 6 units of capital and 4 units of labour and is considering switching to 5 units of capital and 7 units of labour.
   a Calculate the marginal rate of substitution.
   b What factors might the company take into account when considering this substitution?

The meaning of profit 1

Profit can be expressed as:

Profit = total revenue − total costs

where

Total revenue = price per unit sold × quantity sold

Total costs = total fixed costs + total variable costs

However, profit can be seen in a number of ways.

The accountant's view of profit

WORKED EXAMPLE

Turnover (sales revenue) =	£700,000
− Cost of sales =	£250,000
Gross profit =	£450,000

The total cost of sales would include all direct costs such as labour, raw materials and any other costs that are directly related to production. Further deductions are made from gross profit for what are termed **expenses**, which are overheads or fixed costs that are not directly involved with the production of the goods. Such expenses include administrative costs like the wages of the office staff, marketing and advertising expenses, electricity and depreciation.

Thus:

Gross profit =	£450,000
− Expenses =	£200,000
Operating profit =	£250,000

From **operating profit** is deducted any other outgoings, which are usually termed non-operating income or costs. These costs may include rent on premises or interest payments on loans.

Thus:

Operating profit =	£250,000
− Rent/interest payments =	£100,000
Profit before tax =	£150,000

When corporation tax payments are deducted the business is left with profit after tax.

Thus:

$$
\begin{array}{llr}
 & \text{Profit before tax} & = \pounds150{,}000 \\
- & \text{Corporation tax} & = \pounds50{,}000 \\
\hline
 & \text{Profit after tax} & = \pounds100{,}000
\end{array}
$$

The firm may decide to pay out a dividend to its shareholders and in this case decides to distribute £50,000 of the profit as dividends.

Thus:

$$
\begin{array}{llr}
 & \text{Profit after tax} & = \pounds100{,}000 \\
- & \text{Distributed profit} & = \pounds50{,}000 \\
\hline
 & \text{Retained profit} & = \pounds50{,}000
\end{array}
$$

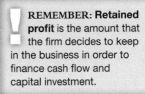

REMEMBER: Retained profit is the amount that the firm decides to keep in the business in order to finance cash flow and capital investment.

PRACTICE QUESTION

1 The table below shows three firms A, B and C.

Firm	A	B	C
Sales revenue (£)	7,500	12,650	25,850
Cost of sales (£)	3,300	5,425	18,613
Expenses (£)	1,500	2,190	3,295

Calculate:

a the gross profit

b the operating profit.

The meaning of profit 2

The economist's view of profit

Normal profit

The definition of **normal profit** is the return required to keep a factor of production in its present occupation. For example, a plumber working on industrial sites may consider that the return he gets for his labour must be £40 per hour. Should his returns fall below this level he may decide to transfer into a different area, e.g. domestic plumbing, in order to return his income to its normal profit levels.

However, unlike accountants, economists include a return that covers the opportunity cost of all factors of production that are involved in production – their normal profit.

✓ WORKED EXAMPLE

A city worker, Emma, is made redundant and decides to turn her hobby into a full-time business, the manufacture of hand-made luxury teddy bears. When the business has been running for a month and teddy bear sales are going well the firm, realising that labour has been too drastically reduced, offers Emma re-employment and gives her seven days to decide whether to continue with the business or return to the office. To reach a conclusion Emma needs to work out whether she will be better off working for the firm or working for herself, and to do this she compiles the following accounts:

	Income from sales (previous month)	= £1,500
−	Cost of raw materials per month	= £450
	Profit	= £1,050

Emma congratulates herself on this level of profit, which would correspond with the accountant's view of gross profit. This is where the accountant's view of profit and that of the economist diverge, as the economist would wish to include opportunity costs as Emma was netting (after tax and national insurance are deducted) £1,500 per month as an administrative worker, and so she is actually £450 per month worse off.

So the true costs of making teddy bears per month must include the £1,500 forgone from city employment giving a revised set of figures:

	Cost of raw materials per month	= £450
+	Income forgone from city	= £1,500
	Total costs	= £1,950

	Income from sales (previous month)	= £1,500
−	Total costs	= £1,950
	Profit (loss)	= − £450

So to reflect the true cost or opportunity cost of producing teddy bears Emma must include the £1,500 that she could have earned in the city.

To cover as a factor of production what she could have earned elsewhere the true cost of teddy bears per month is £1,950 as this includes the normal profit of her labour. Note that if she sells the teddy bears for £1,950, making only normal profit, this implies no hardship as she is making what she could earn elsewhere. However, in this example there are certain other opportunity costs that have not yet been considered:

The room in her house where teddy bears are made could have been let out and yielded an income. The expensive sewing machine that was purchased with her redundancy money could have been leased out and yielded Emma an income. The use of her car to collect the raw materials and transport the finished teddy bears has an opportunity cost as it could have been rented out and earned a return. Finally, we must also include a return to her as an entrepreneur for the worry and stress of running the business: the **entrepreneurial function**. This is extra to the opportunity cost that she could have earned working in the city, as in the city she did not have to face these worries about running the business and risking her own capital.

WORKED EXAMPLE

Continuing the above argument, if we add another £600 for the costs outlined above, the cost of making teddy bears is:

Cost of raw materials per month	=	£450
Income forgone from city	=	£1,500
+ Room, car, stress and worry	=	£600
Total costs	=	£2,550

So the true cost of making teddy bears is £2,550 per month and if Emma receives £2,550 she has covered her normal profit and made as much as she could expect to make elsewhere. This should be sufficient to keep her in her present occupation.

Supernormal profit (SNP)

This is defined as any payment to the firm over and above normal profit and is associated with a monopoly position or the absence of sufficient competition. Supernormal profits can be seen as providing an incentive to firms to enter an industry. They signal entrepreneurs to allocate more factors and therefore are important in allocating scarce resources to areas where they are required.

WORKED EXAMPLE

Assume that in the previous example an exceptional increase in demand for bears increases Emma's revenue to £3,500, while costs remain at £2,550.

Supernormal profit = £3,500 − £2,550 = £950 per month

In the above example, the supernormal profit might be expected to attract other firms or people who can make teddy bears into the industry, as we assume that other firms are making only normal profits. So in the example should Emma's ex-colleagues get to know of this they may decide to embark on teddy bear manufacture themselves. Then these possibilities arise:

- Anyone can make teddy bears in the absence of barriers to entry into the industry, and in response to the supernormal profits others will enter the industry. The supply of teddy bears will then rise and prices will fall, and the supernormal profits will be competed away. People will stop entering the industry when the price has fallen to the point where only normal profits are being made, as they are making normal profits already in their present occupations.
- If making teddy bears is a skill limited to a small number of people, or there are entry barriers to the industry, then others cannot enter and the firm continues to make supernormal profits without worrying about competitors.

Categorisation of profits

- Normal profit is a return that covers the opportunity cost of all factors used in the process of production – the amount necessary to keep a factor in its present occupation.
- Supernormal/abnormal/monopoly profit is a return over and above normal profit.
- Negative or falling profits may indicate that oversupply is taking place and firms will leave the industry and reallocate their factors elsewhere.
- Profits are used by accountants and the media to judge the success of a firm and firms will want to increase their levels of profitability wherever possible.

Perfect competition

A perfect market

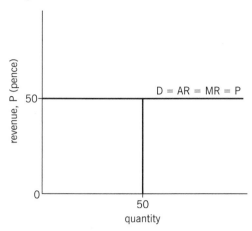 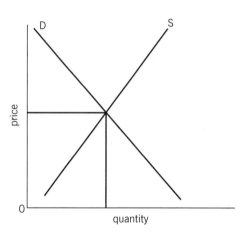

The diagrams above show a **perfect market** where the firm is a **price taker** – it takes its price from the price determined in the market. One of the assumptions of perfect competition is that the firm can sell all it produces at the going price. The demand (D) curve is as a result the horizontal line at price 50p.

$$\text{Average revenue (AR)} = \frac{\text{total revenue (TR)}}{\text{quantity}}$$

 WORKED EXAMPLE

Referring to the diagram above, assuming the firm sells 50 units, the total revenue is the selling price multiplied by output. This is 50p × 50 units = £25.

So average revenue is equal to price.

Marginal revenue (MR) is the revenue received from the sale of one extra unit, and as all units sell for the same price, marginal revenue is also equal to 50p.

Then $\qquad$ P = AR = MR = D

and $\qquad$ $MR_n = TR_n - TR_{n-1}$

where n = the extra unit sold.

Profit maximising output

The diagram opposite illustrates the relationship between marginal cost (MC) and marginal revenue (MR) where the firm's marginal revenue is £50 per unit.

At an output of 1 unit the MC is £20 while the MR is £50, so it clearly pays to supply this unit. Unit number 2 has a marginal cost of £30 but an MR of £50, so is also profitable to produce. Unit 4, however, is another matter as the MC is £80, but the MR is £50, so a profit maximising firm will not produce unit 4 as it adds more to costs than profit.

The firm will not produce beyond unit 3 as at this point MR equals MC.

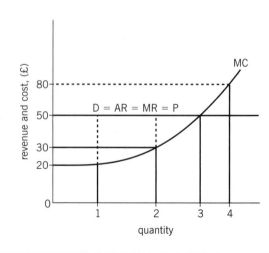

(This is frequently a mystery for students who do not see the logic in selling something for its cost of production. This is a result of the economist's definition of profit (see 'The meaning of profit 2' on page 36).)

The firm will not want to stop production while MR exceeds MC but will not want to produce where MC exceeds MR. Thus:

- When MC > MR, the firm *reduces* output as extra units add more to costs than revenue.
- When MR > MC, the firm *increases* output as extra units add more to revenue that costs.
- When MR = MC, the firm is profit maximising as the unit is adding as much to costs as revenue.

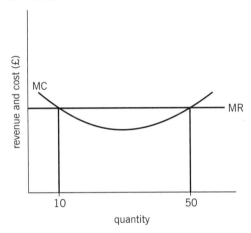

The diagram above shows a slightly different situation as the MR is cut in two places by the MC at an output of both 10 and 50 units. The profit maximising firm will produce at 50 units as units between 10 and 50 add more to revenue than costs. This refines our definition of profit maximisation – a profit maximising firm will produce where marginal revenue equals marginal costs when marginal cost is increasing.

PRACTICE QUESTION

1   A firm is facing a market price of £50 – the table below indicates marginal and average total costs.

Quantity	0	1	2	3	4	5	6	7	8	9
Marginal cost (£)	–	30	20	25	36	50	62	75	89	100
Average total cost (£)		54	45	38	34	38	45	54	65	80

Using the market price:

a   plot the marginal costs curve

b   state the firm's profit maximising output and price

c   calculate the total revenue.

The level of profit or loss

The level of profit or loss is determined by the relationship between the average revenue (AR) curve and the **average total cost (ATC)** curve. The diagram opposite uses the same data as the previous diagrams and the firm's profit maximising quantity is 3 units at £50 per unit. However, at 3 units the total revenue is:

price (AR) × quantity = £50 × 3 = £150

At a quantity produced of 3 units ATC is £40 per unit so ATC × quantity = £40 × 3 = £120

But AR > ATC = **supernormal profit (SNP)** of £10 per unit.

SNP is profit over and above the normal profit that is included in the producer's costs (see 'The meaning of profit 2' on pages 36–7).

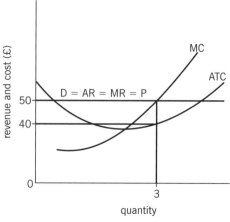

Due to the lack of barriers to entry other firms will enter the industry and in the diagram showing the market the supply curve will shift right and prices will fall until SNP is competed away.

PRACTICE QUESTION

1   Use the data from Question 1 on page 39 to answer the following.
   a   Plot the ATC curve.
   b   What are   i the profit per unit, and   ii the total profit?
   c   Explain what the likely effects are on the industry.

The diagram opposite shows a situation where the firm is making losses. The firm is producing 10 units per week at the profit maximising output (MR + MC) but a comparison of AR and ATC indicates that overall the firm is making a loss.

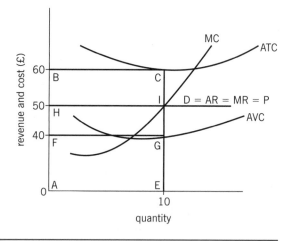

WORKED EXAMPLE

For the above firm,

TR = AR × quantity (Q) = £50 × 10 = £500

TC = ATC × Q = £60 × 10 = £600

∴   TR − TC = −£100

When TC > TR there is negative profit, i.e. a loss, in this case £100.

ATC > AR by £10 per unit.

Firms cannot make losses in the long term and carry on in business, but before shutting down immediately the firm must consider its level of fixed costs. Remember that fixed costs are contractual, e.g. the lease on a building has to be paid until the lease expires or until it can be sold.

WORKED EXAMPLE

Total variable cost (TVC) = average variable cost (AVC) × Q

In the above case, TVC = £40 × 10 = £400.

To work out the average fixed cost (AFC),

AFC = ATC − AVC = £60 − £40 = £20 per unit.

In the diagram areas represent costs as follows:

ABCE = total costs

AFGE = variable costs

FBCG = fixed costs

FHIG = contribution of firm to total costs.

WORKED EXAMPLE

If the above firm closes, the owner will have to pay the full amount of fixed costs. This is given by the area FBCG in the diagram, which is (60 − 40) × (10 − 0) = £200 per week.

However, by continuing in business the firm would only lose an amount given by the area HBCI = (60 − 50) × (10 − 0) = £100 per week.

While the price at which the product sells is above the lowest point of the AVC, it will pay the firm to stay in business to make some contribution to the fixed costs. However, if a major fixed cost comes up for renewal, e.g. the lease on expensive items of capital equipment, the owner may decide this is an opportune time to exit the industry.

PRACTICE QUESTION

Quantity	0	1	2	3	4	5	6	7	8	9
Marginal cost (£)	–	30	20	25	36	50	62	75	89	100
Average total cost (£)					90	75	67	69	75	83
Average variable cost (£)		60	39	25	28	35	43	53		

2　Use the market price of £50 a unit and the table above to answer the following.

   a　Plot the marginal costs curve.

   b　What are the firm's profit maximising output and price?

   c　Calculate the total revenue.

   d　Plot the ATC curve.

   e　What are **i** the profit per unit, and **ii** the total profit?

   f　Plot the average variable costs curve.

   g　Calculate **i** the AFC, and **ii** the TFC.

   h　How much of the TFC is paid by keeping the firm open?

   i　At what price will the firm exit the industry?

Monopoly 1

In the economist's theory of **monopoly** there is only one firm in the industry and the industry demand curve is also the firm's demand curve. In the diagram right, where the demand curve is downward sloping, the marginal revenue and average revenue are not the same.

The demand (D) curve is shown to be equal to the average revenue (AR) curve. The AR is defined as the revenue per unit:

$$AR = \frac{TR}{Q}$$

As TR = P × Q, then

$$AR = \frac{P \times Q}{Q} = P$$

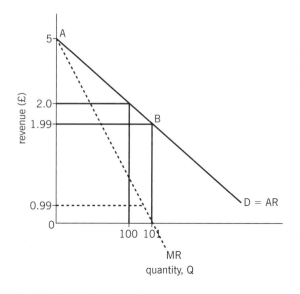

WORKED EXAMPLE

In the diagram above, 100 units are sold at a price of £2, so it follows that the revenue earned per unit (the AR) is also the price of a unit (P), i.e. £2.

The marginal revenue curve

Assume that the firm is selling 100 units at a price of £2 per unit. This means that the total revenue is £200 (= price (AR) × quantity (Q)).

If the firm decides to increase its sales to 101 units, the total revenue increases to £200.99 (= 101 × £1.99).

The marginal revenue is the revenue received from the sale of the extra unit.

WORKED EXAMPLE

In the above case:

marginal revenue = total revenue of 101 units − total revenue of 100 units

$$= £200.99 - £200 = £0.99$$

The reason for this is that in order to sell the extra unit the vendor has had to reduce the price of all previous units by 1p.

 REMEMBER: As a general rule, if a firm faces a negatively sloped demand curve, then at all levels of output P = AR.

Total revenue and marginal revenue

Although the marginal revenue is negatively sloped, it remains positive until it falls below the base line. It follows that when marginal revenue is zero, total revenue is maximised because all marginal revenue added together will equate to total revenue.

Thus $MR_1 + MR_2 + \ldots + MR_n = TR$

This allows us to argue that if price falls from £5 to £1.99 and total revenue is increasing, then demand over the section of the demand curve A to B must be elastic. This is because total revenue increases when price falls and demand is elastic. At any price below £1.99 demand must be inelastic because marginal revenue is negative and is thus reducing the total revenue.

When we considered perfect competition on pages 38–9, you saw that firms will produce where marginal cost equals marginal revenue in order to maximise profits. As marginal costs are likely to be positive, the monopolist will be producing over that part of the demand curve where demand is elastic. A **profit maximising monopoly** will never produce an output in the inelastic range of its demand curve, for if it does so marginal revenue will be negative, and each extra unit sold will reduce total revenue.

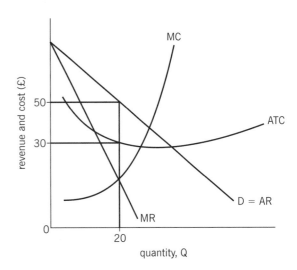

While the monopolist will produce where $MR = MC$, the $MR \neq AR$, and so in the diagram right the price at which the output is sold is obtained where the vertical line drawn from the profit maximising output (20) cuts the AR curve at £50.

The monopolist's total revenue $= AR \times Q = £50 \times 20 = £1000$.

The average total costs can be read off the vertical output line in the same way indicating the ATC $= £30$, giving total costs of ATC $\times Q = £30 \times 20 = £600$.

Total profit $= TR - TC = £1000 - £600 = £400$
Profit per unit $= AR - ATC = £50 - £30 = £20$

As normal profit is included in costs this will constitute the **supernormal profit (SNP)** for the monopolist. Note that with barriers to entry it is unlikely to be competed away.

PRACTICE QUESTION

1 The table below shows the costs and revenue for a monopolist.

Quantity	Demand (AR) (£)	MR (£)	MC (£)	ATC (£)
0		110		
10	104	84	20	68
20	83	56	12	56
30	70	30	30	45
40	55	0	50	43
50	42	–	70	52
60	28	–	–	63
70	14	–	–	–
80	0	–	–	–

a Using the information and graph paper construct the diagram.
b What are i the price and ii the output of the firm?
c Calculate i the total revenue and ii the total costs of the monopolist.
d Calculate the level of SNP earned by the firm.
e At what level of output is the firm's revenue maximised?

Monopoly 2

Monopoly and efficiency

The diagram on the previous page indicates that the monopolist is not **productively efficient** as it does not produce at the lowest point of the ATC curve, and is not **allocatively efficient** as the price of the last unit exceeds the marginal costs of the last unit. This does not preclude **dynamic efficiency** – efficiency over time – if the monopolist uses the supernormal profit (SNP) to invest in research and development and to exploit both the economies of scale and scope (decreases in average costs by increasing the number of goods produced): then the marginal cost shifts downwards as dynamic efficiencies occur as can be seen in the diagram opposite.

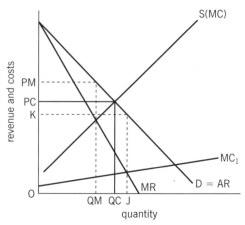

Demand and supply are in equilibrium at OPC and OQC. The diagram can be adapted to show that the industry has been monopolised by the addition of an MR curve and using the existing supply curve as the monopolist's marginal costs curve. Profit maximising output is now OQM at a price of OPM.

If, however, the monopolist uses the resulting SNP to exploit scale and scope efficiencies as well as research and development, it is likely that costs will fall. This is shown by the movement in the marginal costs to MC1, leading to a lower price OK and increased output OJ, and a larger consumer surplus than competition, despite the firm being allocatively inefficient!

PRACTICE QUESTION

1   The table opposite shows the costs and revenue for perfect competition and monopoly.

   a   i Using columns 1, 2 and 3, plot the demand and supply curves and draw in the equilibrium coordinates.

      ii What is the equilibrium price and quantity?

      iii Calculate total revenue.

      iv Calculate the consumer and producer surplus – see 'Taxes and subsidies 2' on page 18.

   b   Assume that the industry is monopolised and the supply curve is now the firm's marginal costs curve.

      i Using column 4, plot the MR curve.

      ii What are the monopolist's price and quantity?

      iii Calculate the total revenue.

      iv Calculate the consumer surplus, producer surplus and welfare loss (see page 18).

Col. 1	Col. 2	Col. 3	Col. 4	Col. 5
Output	**D = AR (£)**	**S = AC (£)**	**MR (£)**	**MC1 (£)**
0				
10	71	12	62	7
20	62	43	44	8
30	54	58	28	9
40	45	64	10	10
50	36	75		12
60	28			13
70	19			14
80	9			16
90	0			

STRETCH YOURSELF

Referring to the table and the answers to Question 1, assume that the monopolist exploits the economies of scale and scope, and marginal costs fall to the level shown in column 5.

   a   Plot the MC curve and draw in the new profit maximising coordinates.

   b   Calculate the revised total revenue.

   c   Calculate the consumer surplus.

   d   Is the monopolist allocatively efficient?

The monopolist's supply curve

A change in demand in perfect competition causes the industry to move along its supply curve and the firm along its MC curve. A change in demand in monopoly causes a change in price and output, and in common with perfect competition the monopolist chooses to equate MR and MC. With competition the marginal costs are equated to price, so the amount supplied at any price is predictable, but with monopoly MC is equated with MR but MR ≠ P so the monopolist does not have a supply curve and this gives rise to the following situations:

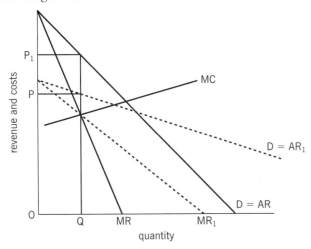
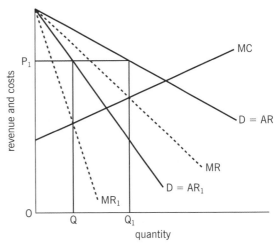

It is not possible to predict how the monopolist will react to a change in demand as the left-hand diagram shows two prices (P and P_1) at one output and the right-hand diagram shows two outputs (Q and Q_1) at one price.

PRACTICE QUESTION

2   The table below shows the monopolist's price and output in two separate markets.

Col. 1	Col. 2	Col. 3	Col. 4	Col. 5	Col. 6	Col. 7
Quantity	QD1 = AR1 (£)	MR1 (£)	QD2 = AR2 (£)	MR2 (£)	MC1 (£)	MC2 (£)
0						
10	75	60	55	50	22	40
20	60	30	50	40	23	51
30	45	0	45	30	25	62
40	30		40	20	27	72
50	15		35	10	28	83
60	0		30	0	30	
70			25		32	
80			20		34	
90			15		36	

a   **i** Using the information in columns 1 to 6, plot the curves.
   ii What are the profit maximising price and output in each market?
   iii What are the revenue maximising quantity and price in each market?
b   Assume that the MC curve shifts to MC2 as shown in column 7.
   i Plot MC2.
   ii What are the new profit maximising output and price in each market?

Imperfect competition 1

Imperfect competition comes in two sizes:
- **monopolistic competition**, in which a large number of small firms comprise the industry
- **oligopoly**, in which a small number of large firms comprise the industry.

Monopolistic competition

Diagrams can be drawn for the short run and long run. The short-run diagram is the same as that for monopoly (see Monopoly 1 on page 43), but there are changes in the long run as there are no barriers to entry to keep other firms out.

The term 'monopolistic' is confusing to students and it needs to be interpreted in terms of localised market power rather than power throughout the whole market.

Another source of confusion is that monopolistically competitive firms differ from perfectly competitive firms because they try to differentiate their product. Rather than seeing this as developing a brand, consider differentiation by location, opening times or staff personality. An example may help: opposite my house are a hairdresser, a Co-op store, a fish and chip shop, an Indian takeaway and a paper shop – they have a monopoly in relation to me because of location, very convenient opening hours and friendly staff, and they remove the need for a car journey in order to purchase. You may see a link here with demand elasticity (see pages 24–5) in that for a relatively small convenience purchase my demand is likely to be inelastic, so price is not a great issue.

First mover advantage should allow supernormal profits (SNP) in the short run – so the first hairdresser in an area should be able to make SNP and will appear as in the left-hand diagram below.

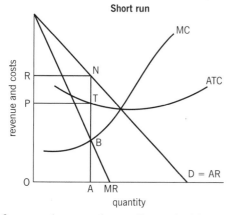

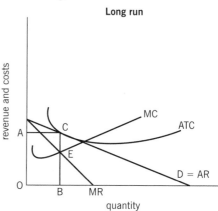

- The firm produces at the profit maximising output OA where MR = MC.
- SNP is given by the area PRNT.
- It is allocatively inefficient because the price of the last unit AN is greater than the MC of the last unit AB.
- It is productively inefficient because the output OA is not at the lowest point of ATC but is underworking the fixed factor at T.
- It is probably too small for dynamic efficiencies, but will try to embrace industry-wide developments to stay competitive, e.g. the hairdresser mentioned above has a 'nail parlour'.

The SNP will attract other firms and in the absence of entry barriers other firms will enter and SNP will be competed away. Then the diagram will appear as in the right-hand diagram above where the demand curve has shifted to the left and become more elastic as consumers now have more choice and existing firms make only normal profit. The existing firms will now have spare capacity because their fixed factors will be underworked (as their ATC will not have fallen as much as demand). The hairdresser's customer base will have shrunk and it will have to find ways to use its spare capacity – perhaps go unisex or modify the premises to offer facials and beauty treatment. Obviously if losses are made it will exit the industry.

- The firm produces at the profit maximising output OB where MC = MR.
- Total revenue = P × Q = OACB; total costs = ATC × Q = OACB, so the firm is making normal profit.
- It is allocatively inefficient because the price of the last unit BC is greater than the cost of the last unit BE.
- It is productively inefficient because the output OB is not at the lowest point of ATC.

However, this may not be the full story as while new entrants may appear they may not be able to physically expand in the same area and the local authority may impose planning limitations. Some firms do develop a localised brand which grows by word of mouth, e.g. it soon gets round that X is a reliable plumber or Z is a very clean plasterer. This suggests that some level of SNP may be possible even in the long run for some firms.

PRACTICE QUESTION

1 The table below shows the costs and revenue curves for a firm in monopolistic competition.

Column 1	Column 2	Column 3	Column 4	Column 5	Column 6	Column 7
Quantity (×1000)	D = AR (£)	MR (£)	MC (£)	ATC (£)	D = AR1 (£)	MR1 (£)
0	110	110	10		60	60
10	98	81	17	65	51	38
20	85	55	23	43	48	18
30	74	29	29	38	34	0
40	60	0	37	35	26	
50	49		44	39	17	
60	37		50	44	9	
70	24		57	55	0	
80	12		64			
90	0					

a Using columns 1–5, plot the short-run diagram for the firm.
b Calculate TR, TC and SNP.

Assume that the firm faces a fall in demand as shown by the figures in columns 6 and 7.

c Calculate the revised profit maximising price and output.
d Assuming that the firm is a taxi company, what action would you advise the business to undertake?

Oligopoly

This is the situation where a small number of firms have most of the market share even though there may be other smaller firms in the industry.

One way of considering the concentration of market share and market power is the **concentration ratio**. (See the diagram of shares and grocery retailing on page 12.) So a ratio of 5 : 70 would mean that the 5 largest firms have 70% of the market share while a concentration ratio of 3 : 70 would mean that the 3 largest firms had 70% of the market share, which would indicate a more highly concentrated market.

PRACTICE QUESTION

2 Using the percentages below:
   a calculate the 3- and 5-firm concentration ratios
   b explain which market is more concentrated and why.

US Truck market

GM	23.4
Toyota	15.9
Ford	15.6
Chrysler	12.6
Honda	9.4
Nissan	6.5
Others	16.6

Video market

Sony	15
Lionsgate	6
Warner	22
Universal	10
Paramount	15
Disney	15
Fox	17

Mobile phone market

Symbian	47
RM	20
iPhone	14
Microsoft	9
Linux	5
Android	4
Web OS	1

Imperfect competition 2

The Herfindahl index

Another measure of concentration is the **Herfindahl index**, which works by squaring the market share for each firm (up to 50 firms) and then summing the squares.

WORKED EXAMPLE

Assume that market share of firms A, B, C and D is as shown here:

The index would be compiled by squaring the firm's market shares:

A = 40%
B = 30%
C = 20%
D = 10%

$40^2 + 30^2 + 20^2 + 10^2 = 1,600 + 900 + 400 + 100 = 3,000$

In a monopoly one firm has 100% of the market, so the index would be $100^2 = 10,000$.

WORKED EXAMPLE

In a situation of perfect competition, assuming that each firm has 0.1% of the market share, then the top 50 firms have an index of $0.1^2 \times 50 = 0.5$.

The calculation can be shown in another form by taking the share of the market and converting it to decimal form.

WORKED EXAMPLE

In the first example above, A = 0.4; B = 0.3; C = 0.2 and D = 0.1.

Squaring each number gives:

$0.16 + 0.09 + 0.04 + 0.01 = 0.3$

This gives a range between 0 and 1. (Perfect competition will actually be just positive).

The result of the calculation is proportional to the average market share, weighted by market share.

The major benefit of the Herfindahl index is that it gives weight to larger firms.

WORKED EXAMPLE

Five firms have 20% of the market each:

$0.2^2 \times 5$ gives an index of 0.2

Now suppose there are 5 firms, of which one has a market share of 80% and the other 4 have 5% each:

$0.8^2 + 4 \times 0.05^2$ gives an index of $0.64 + 0.01 = 0.65$.

The figures resulting from the index can be used to gauge the level of concentration and are used by competition authorities in both the EU and USA.

PRACTICE QUESTION

1 a Using the information from Question 2 on page 47, calculate the Herfindahl index for the 3 markets.
    b Which market is the most concentrated?
    c Which market is the least concentrated?
    d How does your answer differ from the answer to Question 2 on page 47?

Economists characterise oligopoly as exhibiting interdependence and reactive behaviour because firms have to take into account the likely or actual actions of other firms in the industry and have strategies in place to respond or react accordingly. This has given rise to numerous theories, one of which was price 'stickiness' as changing prices could lead to loss of market share if competitors reacted in particular ways. Increasing prices could lead to competitors keeping their prices constant as customers might desert, and lowering prices might provoke a price war – either way the price changer lost out!

This led to the analysis known as the **kinked demand curve** as shown in the left-hand diagram below:

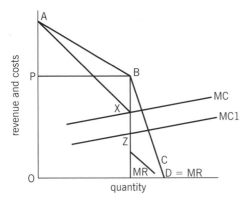

The diagram shows that above the price of OP demand is elastic between A and B on the demand curve, so a firm that raises its price will lose total revenue, while below the price of OP, between B and C on the demand curve, demand is inelastic so the firm will lose revenue if it lowers its price. The MR is discontinuous between X and Z so the MC curve can fluctuate between these points without the firm changing price and output. Using this analysis it is easy to see why an oligopolist may be keen to exploit economies of scale, which will reduce MC to MC1 and increase profits.

While this theory may explain stable prices it does not account for how the price of OP became the benchmark price, and it certainly does not fit the facts for large numbers of oligopolistic industries that compete savagely on price, like supermarkets and cars.

A further consideration is that oligopolists have a choice between competition and collusion to maximise their joint profits rather than their individual profits, and collusion where firms agree to restrict output to a certain level in order to increase prices leads to the possibility of gaining more by cheating.

Game theory

In order to consider this aspect and others in terms of oligopolistic behaviour, economists use **game theory** where firms consider the actions of other firms, their possible responses and the likely possible outcomes of changed behaviour.

The matrix above right shows a situation of two firms in an industry who have agreed to collude.
- If they keep the agreement (top left), both earn £2m.
- If one cheats (top right, bottom left), it earns £5m; the non-cheater loses £1m.
- The Nash equilibrium (bottom right) is that both will cheat.

Both firms on the basis of experience may assume that the other will cheat and it then becomes the strategy that both adopt and make only normal profit. Both firms are better off if they collude rather than compete.

STRETCH YOURSELF

There are two firms A and B in the industry, both considering undertaking investment.

No investment produces returns of £1m.

If one invests and the other does not it receives £3m and the other loses £0.5m.

Both investing produces returns of £1.5m.

With the help of a games theory matrix, explain the possible strategies that the firms might adopt.

The labour market

The supply of labour

The supply of labour to the whole economy consists of all those who are economically active. The economically active are those who are either currently in work or are actively seeking work. Those not actually in work, but actively seeking it, are defined as being unemployed. Those sections of the population that are economically inactive are not part of the labour supply and this number may increase in recession as workers may become 'discouraged' and withdraw from the labour force because they are unable to gain employment. Inactive sections of the population also include students in full-time education, housewives, those who have retired early, prisoners and the severely disabled.

The participation rate, or activity rate, is usually calculated as the percentage of the population in the labour force. The rate is given by the following formula:

$$\text{Participation rate (activity rate)} = \frac{\text{labour force (active population)}}{\text{working-age population}} \times 100$$

$$= \frac{\text{employed} + \text{unemployed}}{\text{working-age population}} \times 100$$

WORKED EXAMPLE

The UK's participation rate was 58% with a total population of 63,227,526.

So the active labour force was:

$(63,227,526 \div 100) \times 58 = 632,275.26 \times 58 = 36,671,965$

What does it show?

- Increasing participation should lead to rising GDP.
- Participation is higher when the benefits of a stronger economy are exhibited in higher wages.
- A more educated society has a higher labour participation rate as those with higher levels of education are less likely to become unemployed or discouraged and drop from the workforce.
- Labour force participation rate does go down as the ratio of senior citizens increases, which will reduce growth rates.

PRACTICE QUESTION

1 Use the figures in the table below to answer the questions.

Country	Participation rate (%)	Total population
Belgium	49	11,142,157
Bosnia	33	3,883,916
France	51	65,696,689
Germany	57	81,889,839
South Africa	39	51,189,307
Spain	44	46,217,961
USA	57	313,914,040

a Calculate the active labour force for each country.
b What further information would be required to explain the different participation levels?

The supply of labour to a particular occupation

The supply of labour to an occupation depends on a mixture of pecuniary (monetary) and non-pecuniary benefits. We often refer to non-pecuniary benefits as 'perks' – aspects of a job that makes it more pleasant, such as long holidays. The analysis of this aspect of labour supply is the theory of **equal net advantage**, which argues that overall reward, taking into account monetary and non-monetary factors, should be equal across the various industries in which a particular occupation could be practised.

For example, consider a 1st class honours economics graduate from a good university who has the choice of staying in academe or joining an investment bank. The rewards may be as follows:

Academe	Investment bank
Reasonable income	Extremely high income
Freedom to direct own research	Work extremely prescribed
Long holidays/reasonably short hours	24/7 always on call
Relaxed working atmosphere	Extremely stressful

If the benefits do not equate then we would expect a transfer of labour from one occupation to another until they are equal. Thus a substantial increase in the salaries of university lecturers could lead to a shift of supply from investment banking to academe.

The labour supply curve

The diagram opposite portrays the framework used to analyse the supply of labour and mentions two effects: the **substitution effect** and the **income effect**.

To understand the relationships it is first necessary to recognise that time can be devoted to leisure or work and each has an opportunity cost in terms of the other. The substitution effect argues that consumers will go for a product whose price has fallen, everything else being equal (*ceteris paribus*).

Thus if income increases, leisure has become more expensive and the real price of goods has fallen because of the rise in income. As a result the substitution effect will lead people to work for longer to get more of the now cheaper goods, so the substitution effect is positive.

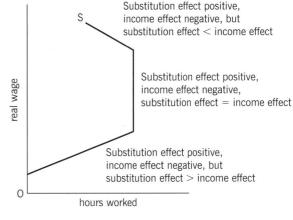

However, as individuals are now richer, they can afford to take more leisure, and this will lead them to reduce their hours, so the income effect is negative.

We argue that the substitution effect is more powerful at low levels of income, and that the two effects are equal over some income range (where the curve is vertical), but the overall effect is negative when income reaches a level where the individual is desperate for leisure. Like most solutions in economics this one comes with provisos in that most employers want full-time workers for stipulated hours, which are contracted and not variable.

PRACTICE QUESTION

2 Which effect, income or substitution, would be dominant in determining whether each of the following went to work on Friday, assuming that they are paid on Thursdays:
  a a factory worker in a repetitive job
  b a managing director of a PLC
  c a nurse
  d a miner
  e a self-employed plasterer?

The elasticity of supply of labour

The **elasticity of supply of labour** measures the responsiveness of the quantity of labour supplied to a change in the real wage rate, and will vary from industry to industry. The formula for elasticity of supply of labour is:

$$\text{elasticity of supply of labour} = \frac{\%\ \text{change in quantity of labour supplied}}{\%\ \text{change in wage rate}}$$

WORKED EXAMPLE

If elasticity of supply of labour is 1.5 it means that a 10% increase in wages will lead to an increase in the supply of labour of $1.5 \times 10\% = 15\%$.

However, an elasticity of 0.2 means that a 10% increase in wages will only produce an increase in the labour supply of $0.2 \times 10\% = 2\%$.

The elasticity of labour supply depends on a number of factors like level of skills required – some jobs, e.g. an engineer, need exceptionally high-level skills, while others, e.g. a cleaner, require less skill. The length of training period will be another factor. For example, it is estimated that it takes 11 years of training to become a consultant surgeon after initially qualifying. Powerful trade unions may be able to make supply more inelastic by limiting the numbers allowed to work in the job.

In terms of diagrams we tend to portray elasticity of supply by the slope of the supply curve, and the diagrams below show both the demand and supply of cleaners and surgeons.

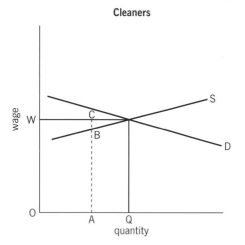

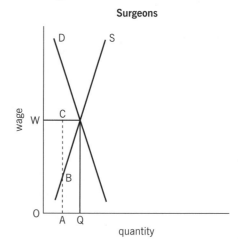

Note that both the demand and supply of cleaners is relatively elastic: demand because most of us are capable of cleaning our own houses, and supply because there are a large number of people who can do the job. With surgeons demand is inelastic: you can't do it yourself and most sane people would not entrust surgery to a friend with a Stanley knife! Supply is inelastic as there are relatively few people who can do the job.

The differing PEOD and PEOS also indicate the difference between **economic rent** and **transfer earnings** for the two groups. Transfer earnings are the payments required to keep a factor in its present occupation – shown as AB in both diagrams, while economic rent is a payment above that of transfer earning shown as BC in the diagrams.

Transfer earnings reflect what a factor could earn in its next best occupation – factors like cleaners with a low MRP would not be likely to have a high level of economic rent whereas factors whose demand and supply is inelastic may earn substantial amounts above what they would earn in their next best occupation. For example, the income of a premiership footballer may be mainly economic rent as their next best occupation is likely to pay a much reduced wage.

It can be seen from the nature of economic rent that it will not affect factor allocation to the economy as the supply to the economy is determined by transfer earnings. Factor OA in the diagrams on page 52 is prepared to work for the wage AB so economic rent is purely a surplus.

WORKED EXAMPLE

Figure 1

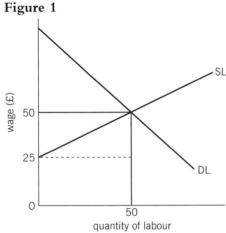

Figure 2

Using Figures 1 and 2 calculate and compare total earnings, economic rent and transfer earnings.

Total earnings in both diagrams are £50 × 50 workers = £2,500

Transfer earnings (Figure 1) = £25 × 50 + $\frac{1}{2}$ × 50 (base) × £25 (height)

$\qquad\qquad$ = £1,250 + £625 = £1,875

Transfer earnings (Figure 2) = $\frac{1}{2}$ × 50 × £50 = 25 × £50 = £1,250

Economic rent (Figure 1) = $\frac{1}{2}$ × £25 (base) × 50 (height) = £12.5 × 50 = £625

Economic rent (Figure 2) = $\frac{1}{2}$ × 50 × £50 = 25 × £50 = £1,250

So while total revenue is the same, transfer earnings and economic rents differ substantially.

PRACTICE QUESTIONS

1 Consider the following occupations:

   painter and decorator $\qquad$ park naturalist $\qquad$ traffic warden $\qquad$ parking lot attendant

   patent lawyer $\qquad$ pathologist (md) $\qquad$ paediatric dentist $\qquad$ bicycle mechanic

   political science professor $\qquad$ postal service clerk $\qquad$ postal service mail carrier.

   Is the elasticity of supply of labour likely to be greater than or less than 1?

2 With the aid of diagrams analyse the effect of an increase in demand for labour in both elastic and inelastic supply.

STRETCH YOURSELF

In 2013 the following premiership football players earned the amounts shown in the table, while a top matron at a hospital earned £56,504 and the average wage level was £26,500.

Rooney	£13.8m
Aguero	£13.5m
Silva	£12.0m
Torres	£10.8m

Using your economic knowledge, account for the differences in income between the various groups.

Examine the case for and against taxing the economic rent in the case of the football players.

Wage determination 1

Wages are determined by a number of factors including demand and supply, the influence of trade unions, professional organisations and government intervention. To analyse the wages paid economists consider labour markets under different conditions.

Perfectly competitive labour markets

Perfectly competitive labour markets make similar assumptions to perfect competition (see pages 38–9). There are a large number of small firms hiring a large number of individual workers, and both firms and workers have to accept the ruling wage. The supply curve of labour is assumed to be perfectly elastic and therefore horizontal, as in the diagram opposite, which means that both the average and marginal cost of labour is the same.

The firm will hire labour at the point where MRP equals the wage paid. As the wage is £200 per week then OA labour will be hired. The average cost of labour is £200 and the marginal cost, the cost of the extra worker, is also £200.

So   SL = AC = MC = W

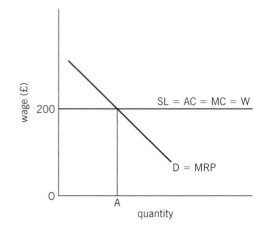

It is often argued that in reality this situation does not exist, but while not all of the assumptions are fulfilled it could approximate to a town that has a flourishing high street and numerous A Level students. The students will know the going rate for working in the town and the shopkeepers will know what they have to pay to attract workers.

PRACTICE QUESTION

1   The table opposite shows the demand and supply of workers at various wage levels.
   a   i   Plot the demand and supply curves shown in columns 2 and 3.
      ii   What is the equilibrium wage?
      iii What is the total wage bill for the employers?
      iv   What are the transfer earnings (see 'The supply of labour' on page 50) for the 20th worker?
      v   What is the economic rent of the 20th worker?
   b   Assume that a large supermarket sets up in the town, leading to the increased demand for labour shown in column 4.
      i   Plot the revised demand curve.
      ii   What is the equilibrium wage?
      iii What are the transfer earnings (see 'The supply of labour' on page 50) for the 20th worker?
      iv   What is the economic rent of the 20th worker?

Column 1	Column 2	Column 3	Column 4
Wage (£)	Demand 1	Supply	Demand 2
0			
1	70		87
2	62		80
3	53		72
4	48	20	65
5	40	40	57
6	32	60	49
7	25	80	42
8	18		34
9	10		

The effect of a trade union

A trade union will try to act as a monopoly seller of labour and seeks to further the interests of its members through a process of 'collective bargaining' with employers. The effect of introducing a trade union on a competitive labour market is shown in the diagram below.

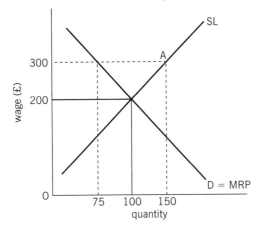

The results can be seen as:

- The trade union increases wage from £200 to £300 per week.
- The supply curve extends along the dotted line from £300 to A and then up the supply curve.
- Demand for workers falls to 75 and their income increases by 50%.
- 25 workers – 76 to 100 – lose their jobs.
- Some of those workers may offer to work for below the union agreed wage.
- 100 to 150 workers offer themselves for work as wages have increased.
- The union has created market failure as unemployment has increased.

PRACTICE QUESTION

2 Using the information from columns 1, 2 and 3 in the table on page 54, assume that the union is successful in imposing a minimum wage of £7.

   a How many workers are now employed?

   b What happens to the firm's total wage bill?

   c How many workers lose their jobs?

   d What is the excess supply of workers?

Wage determination 2

Employers with labour market power

Some firms are known as **monopsonists**, and these are firms that employ a very large percentage of workers in a particular labour market. People who want to be firemen or join the army only have one employer to choose from and that employer is in a position to virtually determine the wage rate. The left-hand diagram below shows two curves: the supply of labour (SL) and marginal cost of labour (MCL).

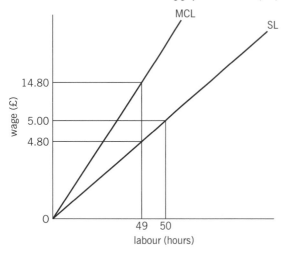
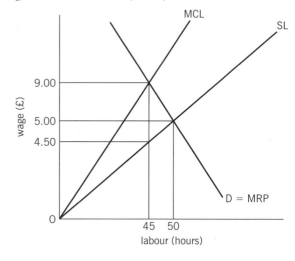

WORKED EXAMPLE

Referring to the diagram (above left) assume that to get 50 hours of work the firm has to pay £5 per hour, giving a total wages bill of $50 \times £5 = £250$.

According to the SL curve the firm can hire 49 hours of work for £4.80 per hour, giving a total wage bill of $49 \times £4.80 = £235.20$.

The extra hour – the marginal cost – has cost the firm $£250 - £235.20 = £14.80$.

The right-hand diagram above has added the monopsonist's demand curve which is equal to the MRP of labour (workers' output × price at which goods sell).

WORKED EXAMPLE

In the right-hand diagram the competitive wage and quantity of labour would be 50 hours at £5 per hour, giving a total wage bill of £250.

The monopsonist will equate the MCL and MRP and hire 45 hours, and pay a supply price of £4.50 per hour.

$\therefore$ Total costs $= £4.50 \times 45 = £202.50$

Thus the monopsonist has saved $£250 - £202.50 = £47.50$ more than would have been possible in a competitive market.

The monopsonist is also making a profit from the labour as the MRP of each hour is £9:

profit per hour $= £9 -$ cost of $£4.50 = £4.50$

$\therefore$ Total profit $= £4.50 \times 45 = £202.50$

Monopsony has led to market failure as fewer workers are employed and at a lower level of wages.

The role of unions and minimum wages

The effect of a trade union on the market will depend on the relative strength of the union compared with the monopsonist. The union is like a monopoly and acts as a single seller of labour. The union is facing a monopsony buyer: a case of a 'bilateral monopoly' where the wage will be determined by bargaining between two traders.

In the right-hand diagram on page 56 consider the union's options:

- It could push to restore the competitive market position – 50 hours at £5 per hour. Note that this would be a case where the union's action would remove market failure.
- It could agree to 45 hours as long as workers were paid their MRP of £9 per hour.
- It could agree to some compromise between 45 and 50 hours.

 WORKED EXAMPLE

The diagram below left shows how the monopsonist's cost curves are constructed when wages increase.

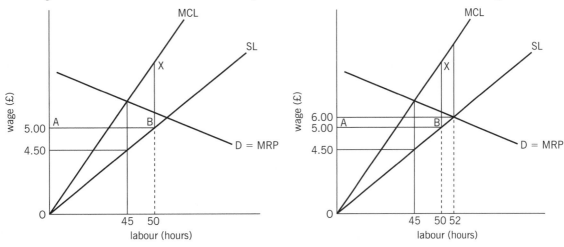

Without a national minimum wage (NMW) the firm employs 45 hours at £4.50 per hour. A NMW is introduced at £5 per hour.

The SL curve shows that £5 per hour must be paid to obtain labour and the new SL curve is horizontal at £5 and proceeds from A to B and then follows the original SL curve.

The MCL curve is also A to B, rises to X and then follows the original MCL curve.

The right-hand diagram above shows that the firm will employ labour as long as the MRP of labour exceeds the MCL of labour. As the NMW rises the firm will employ more labour as long as it does not increase beyond £6 where the MCL cuts the MRP.

 PRACTICE QUESTION

1 The table right gives information regarding a monopsonist employer. Plot the graph and answer the questions.

a What are the competitive wage and hours per week?

b What is the total competitive wage bill?

c How many hours does the monopsonist hire?

d What is the wage paid?

e What is the total wage bill?

f What is the monopsonist's profit per hour?

g Assume a NMW of £4 per hour is imposed. What number of hours will the monopsonist employ?

Labour employed (hours per week)	MRP of labour (£)	Average cost of labour (£)	Marginal cost of labour (£)
10	8.4	0.7	1.4
20	6.8	1.4	2.7
30	5.3	2.0	4.0
40	4.0	2.7	5.4
50	2.3	3.40	6.7
60	0.6	4.0	8.0
70		4.7	
80		5.4	

Increasing labour productivity 1

Productivity

Productivity – the output per worker – tends to be measured over a period of time, usually an hour.

The formula is:

$$\text{Productivity} = \frac{\text{total output}}{\text{total labour force}}$$

It is widely accepted that labour productivity is the key to achieving high long-term growth rates, and unfortunately the UK has tended to score poorly on this front compared with other developed countries.

An example of the importance of labour productivity can be seen in the following example.

Suppose that the output of a factory making sheds is 300 units per month with an employment of 30 workers, each with a selection of the required hand-tools giving a level of productivity of:

$$\frac{300}{30} = 10 \text{ sheds per worker}$$

If the current price of sheds is £750, then the firm's total revenue is £750 × 300 = £225,000.

Assume that total costs represent 40% of the price of the shed. This gives total costs of £225,000 × 0.4 = £90,000.

Assume that 50% of the total costs are wages. Then the total wage bill is £45,000. This gives a current wage per worker of £45,000 ÷ 30 = £1,500. Each worker earns £1,500 per month.

Suppose now that the firm increases its capital equipment by purchasing nail guns to speed up the fixing of the outer cladding to the shed frame and that 300 units can now be made with 25 workers.

Productivity has increased to $\frac{300}{25} = 12$ sheds per worker

The wage per worker can be increased to £45,000 ÷ 25 = £1,800 per month. The workers' MRP has increased (see page 56).

Now assume that the firm introduces an assembly line, where each worker receives improved technology relevant to the part of the job that he is performing, so that those workers who make the frame now have technology that can cut the joints to precise accuracy, which will improve the quality of the product.

Productivity now increases, as only 20 workers are now required to produce 300 sheds per month. Thus £45,000 can now be shared among 20 workers increasing wages to £2,250.

Let us assume that because of the advanced technology the firm's product is of a superior quality, which allows it to either:

- sell more sheds at the existing price, or
- increase the price at which it sells its sheds.

Suppose the firm decides to increase the price to £825, which will increase total revenue to £247,500: an improvement of £22,500. Assuming that total wage costs remain the same at £45,000, profits will increase by £22,500 and if wages are left at the same level, then wages as a percentage of total revenue have fallen from 25% to 18%:

$$£45,000 \div £247,500 \times 100 = 18\%$$

The firm has gained from an increase in its profit levels and a fall in the percentage paid to labour.

PRACTICE QUESTIONS

1 A fall in the price of raw materials causes the above firm's total costs to fall to £40,000. New technology reduces the amount of labour required by the firm to 16 workers. Assuming that total revenue remains constant, calculate:

   a labour productivity

   b the wages that the workers could receive, assuming wages are 25% of total costs

   c the profits earned by the firm.

2 The firm now increases the price of sheds to £850. Calculate:

   a the revised total revenue

   b the revised figures for 1a and c above.

However, there are further benefits to be had. So far the firm has reduced the number of workers required for shed building by 10 workers, and an assumption often made is that technological improvements will lead to unemployment, as the firm now needs fewer workers to build its sheds. This is what economists call the 'lump of labour' fallacy: that there are only a certain number of jobs to go round. The firm may decide that it can now expand its range of products and go into the production of dog kennels with the labour that is no longer making sheds.

An alternative is that the labour is now freed up to work in another part of the economy, and in so doing increases output and therefore the rate of economic growth.

It is clear that improvements in productivity will increase growth rates in the long run, although there may be some unemployment in the short run as displaced workers seek other employment.

Increasing labour productivity 2

Multifactor productivity (MFP)

Multifactor productivity (MFP) aims to consider all the factors of production and includes technological progress, the effect of changes in management techniques and business processes and more efficient use of factor inputs. MFP reflects how factor inputs are employed.

An increase in MFP means that more output is obtained from the same set of inputs, or equivalently that fewer inputs can be used to make the same amount of output. This can occur because new technology is adopted or because inputs are utilised more efficiently. This is a management function, the implication being that efficient management will take advantage of the availability of new knowledge, or greater effort will take advantage of existing knowledge. Managers achieve this by trying to reduce costs, develop better products, and imitate cost–effective production processes introduced by their rivals. This activity, which economists call **dynamic efficiency**, will increase MFP.

$$\text{Multifactor productivity} = \frac{\text{total output}}{\text{KELMS}}$$

where

K = £ quantity of capital
E = energy (not used in all calculations)
L = £ quantity of labour
M = £ quantity of materials
S = £ quantity of business services (managers).

WORKED EXAMPLE

The table opposite shows the total costs of various factors and in column 1, given the mix of factor proportions, total costs are £121,250. If the firm's total output is £247,500,

then $\quad \text{MFP} = \dfrac{247,500}{121,250} = 2.04$

Factor	Column 1 (£)	Column 2 (£)	Column 3 (£)
Capital	10,000	15,000	8,000
Labour	33,750	28,000	36,000
Materials	27,500	25,000	25,000
Management	50,000	40,000	40,000
Total	121,250	108,000	

In column 2 the factor combinations have been adjusted following an efficiency review, which suggested increasing capital and reducing the proportions of labour and management. The review also found wastage of raw materials.

So $\quad \text{MFP} = \dfrac{247,500}{108,000} = 2.29$

This represents an increase in total factor productivity (TFP) of 0.25.

It is fairly clear that productivity of factors is likely to affect workers' pay levels and employment possibilities, but it may be that wages can affect productivity. Nominal wages in the UK since 2007 have risen by about 1.6% per year while inflation has averaged 3%, leading to a fall in real wages over the period of 7.8%. This may explain why firms are now hiring workers, as falling real wages leads to more labour and less capital being employed. This will have an effect on productivity (= total output/total labour force) as an increase in the total labour force relative to capital will see labour productivity fall.

This situation may be contrasted with the USA where unemployment has not fallen so rapidly. In the USA real wages have risen by about 2% because of mild inflation. This may discourage firms from hiring more labour but lead to them trying to increase the productivity of the existing workforce.

PRACTICE QUESTION

1   In column 3 of the table on page 60 the firm has employed extra labour as real wages have fallen and not replaced some of its worn out capital equipment.
   a   Calculate the MFP.
   b   Examine the possible long-term effects on the firm.
   c   Evaluate the likely effects on an economy of adopting the UK or USA approach.

Determinants of productivity

Investment in physical capital

Economists tend to examine the increase in capital equipment from two perspectives:

- **Capital widening** where the increase in capital input occurs at the same rate as the increase in labour input so that the proportion in which capital and labour are combined to produce output is unchanged. This can be seen initially in the example where each worker was provided with a set of hand-tools, and if extra workers had been employed they would also have been provided with the same equipment.
- **Capital deepening** where the increase in capital input is faster than the increase in labour input so that proportionately more capital than labour is used. This occurs when the firm increases its capital equipment by using machinery, which requires less labour.

New technology

The term 'new technology' implies technology that is superior to that which is currently being used. It makes capital equipment more efficient and thus increases productivity. You have grown up with what my generation sees as revolutionary technology: the transformation, transmission and dominion of information in which services like Skype have transformed communication. Also modern technology has provided ways to grow more food, transport more people and make more products for a growing society. One of the biggest benefits of modern technology is that human health has improved because of its application.

The rapid economic growth of Japan after World War II and of the East Asian 'tigers' – Singapore, Hong Kong, Taiwan, and South Korea – in the 1990s was largely a result of their ability to adopt new technologies quickly, such as the internet and innovative steelmaking processes. Other countries like those in Latin America, which were relatively slow in their adoption of these same technologies, saw a drop in per capita income over the same periods.

Investment in human capital – education and training

We have seen on pages 54–7 that MRP determines a worker's wage, and in general well-trained workers tend to be more productive and earn more money than workers with poorer training. An economy with trained labour has a workforce capable of operating at a level where it holds a competitive advantage over the economies of other countries.

A country's economy becomes more productive as the proportion of educated workers increases because educated workers are able to carry out jobs that require literacy and critical thinking. As a result countries with a greater proportion of their population attending and graduating from schools see faster economic growth than countries with less educated workers.

The more educated well-trained workers a firm employs, the more the firm can theoretically produce. An economy in which employers treat education as an asset in this manner is often referred to as a **knowledge-based economy**.

Management

Managers are responsible for providing incentives in terms of pay, working conditions and working practices that incentivise the workforce. They also need to be able to appreciate and employ the most efficient combination of factors of production.

Gross domestic product

In order to decide how the economy is performing in terms of its macro objectives and how it compares with other economies the government uses 'indicators', which are items of data that show different aspects of the economy's performance. Economic indicators are statistics that provide information about the expansion and contraction of business cycles, and the one used to measure economic growth is **gross domestic product (GDP)**.

GDP is used to measure the value of all goods and services produced in the economy by the three wealth creating sectors: manufacturing, agriculture and the service industries. It is usually expressed in three ways that you will probably have encountered in your study of the circular flow of income:

- the total value of output
- the total value of expenditure
- the total value of incomes.

Given some small statistical differences the value of the three measures should be broadly similar.

There is a distinction between GDP and **gross national product (GNP)**. GDP is the total value of all goods and services produced in a country over a period of say a year irrespective of who owns the factors of production. GNP is GDP plus income earned from domestic firms abroad minus income earned by foreign firms located in the country under consideration.

National income (NI) is the output produced by resources within the UK, plus net property income from abroad, minus depreciation of the nation's capital equipment.

In summary:

GDP + net property income from abroad = GNP

GNP − depreciation of capital equipment = NI

To calculate **nominal GDP** (GDP in monetary terms) from expenditure we add together the factors that constitute **aggregate demand**, i.e. consumption + investment + government expenditure + (exports minus imports).

WORKED EXAMPLE

The table below shows data for a country. The figures for GDP are complete for the year 2000.

Copy the table and fill in the gaps to complete the nominal GDP figures.

Component	2000 (£bn)	2001 (£bn)	2002 (£bn)	2003 (£bn)
Consumption (C)	600	650	700	
Investment (I)	50	75	81	90
Government expenditure (G)	255	240		290
Exports (X)	400	500	450	430
Imports (M)	480		500	530
Total GDP (£bn)	825	815	1,006	1,030

Answer: GDP = C + I + G + (X − M). Substituting the figures in this equation gives:

Component	2000 (£bn)	2001 (£bn)	2002 (£bn)	2003 (£bn)
Consumption (C)	600	650	700	**750**
Investment (I)	50	75	81	90
Government expenditure (G)	255	240	**275**	290
Exports (X)	400	500	450	430
Imports (M)	480	**650**	500	530
Total GDP (£bn)	825	815	1,006	1,030

While either the GDP or GNP may give an idea as to the size of the economy compared with others, it does not provide information about the amount that each person in the economy has available to spend, i.e. the spending power of the average person. For most economies the spending power of the individual, or **GDP per capita**, is a much better indicator of the population's standard of living than total GDP because it takes into account the population size. Countries can have similar total GDPs but with large differences in population size.

In order to calculate GDP per capita, the GDP is divided by the population to obtain the amount available to the average person to spend.

However, the GDP per capita figure is an average and there may be huge differences in the level of income throughout some economies, especially emerging economies where some may live in splendour while others live in abject poverty. In this case GDP per capita does not give much of an indication of average purchasing power.

WORKED EXAMPLE

According to government statistics, nominal GDP for 2011 was £1,507,585 million and GDP per capita was £24,005. What was the population size?

$$\frac{£1,507,585}{X} \text{ million} = £24,005$$

where X is the population size.

Therefore

$$X = \frac{£1,507,585}{£24,005} \text{ million} = 62.80 \text{ million (to 2 decimal places)}$$

PRACTICE QUESTION

1 Use the table below.

Country	GDP ($)	Population
Angola	475,501,675,733	20,820,525
Austria	394,707,863,204	8,462,446
Bermuda	5,473,536,000	64,806
Cameroon	25,321,590,402	21,699,631
Central African Republic	2,184,181,391	4,525,209
Chile	269,869,337,788	17,464,814

a Calculate GDP per capita.

b Do these figures reflect household purchasing power?

Nominal and real GDP

GDP measures the value of goods and services traded in the market place, where the value of the goods is arrived at by multiplying the price at which they sell by the quantity. However, there is a problem with the nominal figure this gives us because we do not know whether the output of the goods and services has increased, or their prices have risen, or whether an output increase is coupled with a price rise. To determine the actual increase in the real (physical) output of goods and services we need to eliminate any inflationary price increase that would increase the **nominal** (monetary output) but not **real** output.

To convert **nominal GDP** to **real GDP** we use the price index for the relevant year known as a **price deflator** or **GDP deflator**. The formula for calculating real GDP is:

$$\text{Real GDP} = \frac{\text{nominal GDP}}{\text{price index}} \times 100$$

WORKED EXAMPLE

Using price index (deflator) values of 103 for the year 2009 and 105.8 for the year 2010, and assuming the figures are in billions of pounds, then in the year 2009 the nominal value of GDP was £1,220bn and in 2010 it was £1,251bn.

Calculate the real GDP for 2009 and 2010.

Using the formula:

$$\text{Real GDP in 2009} = \frac{1,220}{103} \times 100 = £1,184.5\text{bn}$$

$$\text{Real GDP in 2010} = \frac{1,251}{105.8} \times 100 = £1,182.4\text{bn}$$

Goods and services	Quantity of units in basket (weights)	Prices of goods in base year 2008 (£)	Value of goods in base year 2008 (£)	Quantity of goods in 2009 (weights)	Real value of goods in 2009 (£)	Quantity of goods in 2010 (weights)	Real value of goods in 2010 (£)
DVDs	12	2.5	30	14	35	16	40
Food	35	20	700	33	660	38	760
Transport	12	8	96	14	112	14	112
Leisure	8	7	56	7	49	9	63
Hairdressing	6	5	30	6	30	8	40
Clothes	15	18	270	14	252	19	342
Total value of basket			1,182		1,138		1,357

The table above uses the same base year as in the example above, but here the quantities of goods in 2009 and 2010 are multiplied by the prices of the goods in the base year. Thus in 2009, 14 DVDs are multiplied by the base year price of £2.50 and so on throughout the table. As a result the real GDP becomes a measure of output at unchanging prices.

Calculating the GDP deflator

Given both nominal and real figures for GDP we can calculate the GDP deflator by rearranging the formula for real GDP given on page 64:

$$\text{GDP deflator} = \frac{\text{nominal GDP}}{\text{real GDP}} \times 100$$

WORKED EXAMPLE

Using the figures in the table on page 64, calculate the GDP deflator for the years 2009 and 2010.

For 2009:

$$\text{GDP deflator} = \frac{1{,}220}{1{,}138} \times 100 = 107.21$$

For 2010:

$$\text{GDP deflator} = \frac{1{,}251}{1{,}357} \times 100 = 92.19$$

So in 2009 prices rose by 7.2% compared to the base year, whereas in 2010 they fell by 7.81% when compared with the base year. The latter is a situation of deflation.

PRACTICE QUESTION

1   With the aid of the nominal GDP figures for 2001 to 2003 from the example on page 62, work out:

    a the GDP deflator for 2000 if real GDP was £790bn

    b the real income for 2001 if inflation was 3%

    c the GDP deflator for 2002 with a real GDP figure of £1,256bn

    d the real income for 2003 if inflation was 5.5%.

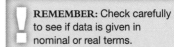

REMEMBER: Check carefully to see if data is given in nominal or real terms.

GDP and welfare

GDP has often been used to measure economic welfare but either in nominal or real form it is a very limited indicator and economists have developed other measures of welfare.

The following quote from economist Mark Anielski indicates in humorous form the limitations of GDP:

'The ideal economic or GDP hero is a chain-smoking terminal cancer patient going through an expensive divorce whose car is totaled in a 20-car pileup, while munching on fast-take-out-food and chatting on a cell phone. All add to GDP growth. The GDP villain is non-smoking, eats home-cooked wholesome meals and cycles to work.'

STRETCH YOURSELF

Research and compare alternative measures of economic welfare.

Consumption, saving and expenditure

The left-hand diagram below shows the relationship between consumption, saving and income. Consumption increases as income and real GDP rise, and is positive at OB even when income is zero. Saving is negative at low levels of income below OA and then increases as income rises. Consumption can be divided into two components: **autonomous** and **induced** expenditure.

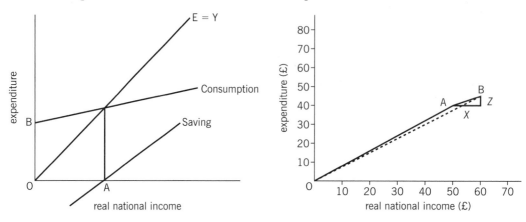

Autonomous and induced expenditure

- **Autonomous expenditures** are those components of expenditure that do not vary with real national income. On the diagram they are shown by OB, where real national income is zero.
- **Induced expenditure** is that part of consumption that changes as income changes and on the diagram it can be seen that, while autonomous expenditure remains at B, induced expenditure rises with income.

The diagram shows that from O to A, consumption exceeds income and that saving is negative. People are consuming more than their income by dissaving, spending past savings, receiving charity or stealing what they require.

The **average propensity to consume (APC)** is the proportion of income spent on consumption:

$$APC = \frac{C}{Y}$$

The **marginal propensity to consume (MPC)** is the proportion of extra income spent on extra consumption:

$$MPC = \frac{\Delta C}{\Delta Y}$$

On the diagram, at incomes beyond OA savings become positive as income increases, showing that the relationship between consumption and savings changes as income changes. Thus both the MPC and the marginal propensity to save (MPS) also change. The slopes of the curves in the diagram are the marginal propensities.

PRACTICE QUESTION

1 The table below shows a change in income over a four-year period.

Year	Income (£)	Consumption (£)	APC	MPC
1	10,000	9,800		
2	12,000	11,100		
3	15,000	12,200		
4	20,000	14,500		

Calculate:

a the APC for each year   b the MPC for years 2, 3 and 4.

From the diagram we can see that APC > Y at low levels of income, and APC = 1 at the break-even point then falls as a proportion of income.

MPC < 1 at all levels of income, but may be a constant or declining percentage of income.

The right-hand diagram on page 66 shows a graph of the **consumption function**. Income is measured on the x-axis and expenditure on the y-axis. Point A represents a situation where income is £50 and expenditure is £40.

WORKED EXAMPLE

Referring to the diagram, the APC is at A given by the slope of the line OA. This is the vertical distance 40 ÷ the horizontal distance 50, i.e.

APC at A = 40 ÷ 50 = 0.8

Similarly, the APC at B is equal to the slope of OB (shown as a broken line), i.e.

APC at B = 45 ÷ 60 = 0.75

The MPC is $\Delta C \div \Delta Y$.

Graphically ΔC is the distance Z (= 50 − 45 = 5) and ΔY is the distance X (= 60 − 50 = 10), so MPC is the slope of AB.

∴   MPC = 5 ÷ 10 = 0.5

PRACTICE QUESTION

2   a   Draw a graph similar to the left-hand one on page 66 with expenditure and income running from zero to 70.

   b   Plot points where Y = 20 and C = 20; Y = 40 and C = 40; and Y = 70 and C = 70.

   c   Compare APC and MPC at these three positions.

   d   Join the points on a new straight line with coordinates Y = 0, C = 20; Y = 50, C = 35; and Y = 70, C = 40.

   e   Calculate the MPC between £30 and £40, and between £60 to £70.

   f   At what point are consumption and income equal?

   g   Plot the savings schedule (= Y − C).

The aggregate consumption function

If all households had the same marginal propensity to consume, then redistribution of income by taxing some and giving benefits to others would not affect the level of **aggregate consumption**: what was lost in tax, and thereby consumption, would be received by others as benefits and spent. But given that as incomes rise consumption as a proportion of income falls, or looking at it the other way round that richer households can save more than poorer households, then aggregate consumption is likely to change if incomes are redistributed.

WORKED EXAMPLE

Taxing a household with an MPC of 0.6 and giving it to a household with an MPC of 0.8 will increase spending by:

0.8 − 0.6 = £0.20, i.e. 20p in every pound redistributed.

This would lead to a rise in national income.

Price index 1

Constructing a price index

The Consumer Price Index attempts to measure the average price level of goods and services that a typical UK household consumes – the average level of inflation. The index is constructed on the basis of a 'basket' of goods consumed by the average household. The authorities collect information on expenditure patterns through the 'Living costs and food survey', which indicates what proportion of household expenditure is spent on particular goods and services. This allows the items in the survey to be 'weighted' according to their importance in expenditure patterns. The authorities choose a base year where the index is given the value of 100 as any price changes after that year can easily be expressed as a percentage.

In the past prices were collected by a team of observers from 180 locations around the country but this operation can now be performed by using the internet rather than actual visits.

The table below shows the construction of a part of a hypothetical index. The columns have been numbered to enable ease of reference.

Column 1	Column 2	Column 3	Column 4	Column 5	Column 6	Column 7	Column 8
Goods and services	Quantity of units in basket (weights)	Prices of goods in base year (2008) (£)	Value of goods in base year (2008) (£)	Prices of goods in 2009 (£)	Value of goods in 2009 (£)	Prices of goods in 2010 (£)	Value of goods in 2010 (£)
DVDs	12	2.5	30	3.0	36	3.25	39
Food	35	20	700	22	770	23	805
Transport	12	8	96	9	108	9	108
Leisure	8	7	56	7.50	60	8.5	68
Hairdressing	6	5	30	6	36	6	36
Clothes	15	18	270	14	210	13	195
Total value of basket			1,182		1,220		1,251

Column 1 refers to the goods and services that would be put into the basket. A possible limitation here is that with new goods and services entering the market so rapidly the index may lag behind what households actually spend their incomes on. Other goods may 'fall out' of the index as they are unimportant in consumers' spending patterns.

Column 2 refers to the 'weighting' of the goods in the basket according to the percentage of household income spent on them. As not all goods are equally important weighting is necessary.

 WORKED EXAMPLE

Suppose that households spend 60% of their income on food and 40% on transport. If there is a 6% increase in the price of food and a 4% increase in the price of transport a simple average would add 6% to 4% and divide the result by 2 leading to an average price increase of 5%.

This would be inaccurate as food spending is a larger proportion of income than transport spending, so weighting is required. Food makes up 60% of household expenditure (= 0.60) while transport is 40% (= 0.40).

The price increase for food is 6% × 0.60 = 3.6%

The price increase for transport is 4% × 0.40 = 1.6%

The average price increase is 3.6% + 1.6% = 5.2%.

If the CPI was 100 at the beginning of the year it would have increased to 105.2 by the end of the year.

Column 3 shows the prices of the goods in the index in the base year of 2008.

Column 4 shows the total value of the goods in the base year (weight × price). This is calculated by taking the quantity of the individual goods, e.g. 12 DVDs (column 2) and multiplying them by the relevant price – £2.50 (column 3) in the case of DVDs – giving a total of £30 in column 4. The value of the individual goods in column 4 is then summed to give the total of £1,182.

Column 5 shows the price changes that have occurred during 2008 and gives a revised figure for 2009.

Column 6 is calculated in the same manner as column 4, e.g. 12 DVDs at £3 give a value of £36 in column 6. The value of the individual items is then summed to give a figure of £1,220.

Column 7 shows the price changes that have occurred in 2009 to give a revised figure for 2010.

Column 8 shows the individual and total value of goods in 2010.

To calculate the price index for a particular year we use the formula:

$$\text{price index for a particular year} = \frac{\text{value of basket in a particular year}}{\text{value of same basket in the base year}} \times 100$$

WORKED EXAMPLE

The price index numbers for the years in the table on page 68 are

For 2008:

$$\text{Price index} = \frac{1,182}{1,182} \times 100 = 1 \times 100 = 100$$

For 2009:

$$\text{Price index} = \frac{1,220}{1,182} \times 100 = 1.032 \times 100 = 103.2$$

For 2010:

$$\text{Price index} = \frac{1,251}{1,182} \times 100 = 1.058 \times 100 = 105.8$$

Thus average prices increased by 5.8% between 2008 and 2010.

> **REMEMBER:** While calculation from the base year is relatively straightforward care must be taken when calculating the percentage change between years, e.g. years 2009 and 2010, as it is not simply the numerical difference between 105.8 and 103.
>
> The percentage change calculation must be worked out:
>
> $$\text{percentage change} = \frac{\text{final number} - \text{initial number}}{\text{initial number}}$$
>
> In the above case:
>
> $$\text{percentage change} = \frac{105.8 - 103.2}{103.2} \times 100$$
>
> $$= \frac{2.6}{103.2} \times 100 = 2.52\%$$
>
> So the rate of inflation between 2009 and 2010 was 2.52% but between 2010 and the base year it was 5.8%.

PRACTICE QUESTION

1 The following table shows the quantities and prices consumed for the years 2008 to 2010.

Goods and services	Quantity of units in basket (weights)	Prices of goods in base year (2008) (£)	Value of goods in base year (2008) (£)	Prices of goods in 2009 (£)	Value of goods in 2009 (£)	Prices of goods in 2010 (£)	Value of goods in 2010 (£)
Food	25	100		102		105	
Housing	25	80		85		90	
Transport	15	10		9		9.5	
Clothing	15	12		14		13.5	
Leisure	10	4		9		9.5	
Other items	10	10		14		13	
Total value of basket	100						

   a Calculate the value of the goods in the years 2008, 2009 and 2010.

   b Calculate the price index between the base year and 2010.

   c What was the increase in price index between 2009 and 2010?

Price index 2

The index on the previous page was increasing over time and thus shows an increasing level of prices or inflation. If the index falls in value, going forward in time, it shows deflation:

2000	2001	2002	2003	2004
92.3	97.2	100	106.9	105.4

In the period 2000–2003 prices on average increased, but in 2004 prices fell. Here 2002 is the base year.

In 2000 and 2001 average prices were lower than in the base year as the indices are below 100.

Note that you could be presented with figures where the base year is not the initial year shown. For the calculations to be meaningful they must be calculated on the basis of the same base year and basket of goods. Thus the figures in 2000 and 2001 will have been calculated from a previous base year and will not be related to years 2002 to 2004.

Nominal and real value

In economics we measure output in terms of **value**, which is defined in monetary terms, i.e. the quantity of a good or service produced multiplied by the price. **Nominal value** is the monetary value of a particular good or service. For example, if you pay £10 to have your windows cleaned the nominal value (what you have paid) is £10. So calculations of income output and expenditure can be expressed in nominal terms, as can the price of money, the rate of interest.

However, when the value of output increases the question arises whether the increase represents an increase in physical output – more actual goods and services – or just a price increase in existing goods and services, or a combination of both increased output and increased prices.

To eliminate the effect of increased prices and obtain the **real value** of any increase we must eliminate the influence of price changes.

> **REMEMBER:** As you can imagine it is very important to use real price measures when comparing statistics across different countries that may have different rates of inflation.

Nominal and real interest rates

It is also worth pointing out the difference between **nominal** and **real interest rates:**
- **Nominal interest rates** are not adjusted for inflation.
- **Real interest rates** have been adjusted for inflation.

The real interest rate is more important for businesses and consumers when they make decisions about spending and saving. The real rate of return on savings, for example, is the nominal rate of interest minus the rate of inflation. So, if savers receive a nominal rate of interest of 5% on their savings, but price inflation is 2%, the real rate of return on these savings is only 3%.

The figures opposite cover a past period of inflation in the UK economy, but illustrate the need to appreciate the difference between nominal and real:

Year	Price index
1974	100
1977	182
1978	197
1979	223
1980	263

The base year is 1974, so the value of the index is 100. During the period 1974 to 1980 the price index increased from 100 to 263, an increase of 163. This meant that the yearly average rate of inflation was 163 ÷ 6, i.e. about 27% per annum. To put this another way, the value of money fell by 27% per year!

Price indices, by showing both inflation rates and falls in the value of money, enable individuals to work out whether they are better or worse off over a period of a year, and what is happening to the value of their savings.

The above figures considered in today's terms would be thought of as extremely high, because during the period interest rates reached a maximum of 17.5%. However, savers would have been experiencing a fall in the value of their savings as they may have received 17.5% on their deposits in banks but the value of their money was falling by 27% per year. While the nominal rate of interest was positive, savers were receiving a negative return on their savings.

The nominal rate of interest was 17.5%, but the real rate of interest is the nominal rate of interest adjusted for inflation. The real rate of interest was 17.5%, (the nominal rate) minus inflation 27%, which equals the real rate of interest, minus 9.5%.

Whenever the level of inflation exceeds the nominal rate of interest real interest rates will be negative.

PRACTICE QUESTION

1 Use the table below to answer the following.

Year	Price index
2009	100
2010	104.4
2011	98.9
2012	97.3
2013	105.2
2014	103.7

a Calculate the real return on an annual deposit with a nominal interest rate of 8%.

b In which years would a nominal 3% interest rate give a real return?

c If house prices grew in real terms by 10% over the period 2009–14, would the investor have been better off investing in housing?

The Keynesian multiplier 1

Two-sector economy

An increase in any of the components of aggregate demand, AD $(= C + I + G + (X - M))$, will not only increase the size of GDP but produce a result larger than the initial expenditure. The reason for this is the **Keynesian multiplier** effect.

A simple example will illustrate this:

Consider a **two-sector economy**, such as you came across when studying the circular flow of income (see page 66), with one injection (investment) and one withdrawal (saving). In this economy the multiplier works in the following way:

- Assume that the level of national income is in equilibrium and that a business invests £10m in new machinery.
- Injections are now greater than withdrawals by £10m and national income will start to increase.
- National income is now in disequilibrium as investment is greater than saving.
- National income will increase until investment and saving are equal.
- Assume that people save $\frac{1}{5}$ of their extra income. We say that the **marginal propensity to save (MPS)** is $\frac{1}{5}$. This means that the **marginal propensity to consume (MPC)** is $1 - \frac{1}{5} = \frac{4}{5}$.
- When national income has risen by £50m then $\frac{1}{5}$ will be saved and $\frac{1}{5}$ of £50m is equal to £10m, which equals the original injection.

The formula for the Keynesian multiplier is:

$$\text{multiplier (K)} = \frac{\text{change in GDP}}{\text{initial change in investment}}$$

WORKED EXAMPLE

In the simple case above,

$$K = \frac{£50m}{£10m} = 5$$

If the above formula is rearranged we get:

change in GDP = initial change in investment $\times$ multiplier (K) = £10m $\times$ 5 = £50m

The multiplier effect is due to the initial expenditure producing a chain of further expenditure and employment, which in turn generate further income, expenditure and employment. Thus in the case above the business decided to invest in new machinery. This provides income for workers in the capital goods industry who will receive the payment for making the machinery, and they will spend this money on consumer goods and services that will create further employment. This is known as **induced spending** because it is caused by the change in GDP. The newly employed workers in other businesses will receive money, which they will spend, so the initial injection will continue to generate demand and have an effect far greater than the original injection.

However, to calculate the true value of the multiplier we must also note that consumers do not spend all of the extra money they receive. Therefore the multiplier effect cannot continue forever, because at each stage of the circular flow of money some of the money received will leave in the form of **leakages**: it will be withdrawn, in the form of taxes, savings, or spending on imports. In the case of a two-sector economy the only leakage is saving.

WORKED EXAMPLE

In the case above the MPS was $\frac{1}{5}$, which means that $\frac{1}{5}$ is leakage, and consumption (MPC) is $1 - \frac{1}{5} = \frac{4}{5}$ of total income. This can be seen in the following table.

In the table, assuming that the MPC is $\frac{4}{5}$ of the initial increase in spending of £10m, we have:

induced expenditure = $\frac{4}{5} \times$ £10m = £8m

This £8m becomes the change in income in the second round, where once again $\frac{4}{5}$ is spent and $\frac{1}{5}$ saved, giving an increase in induced expenditure of £6.4m.

This process continues with the induced expenditure progressively becoming smaller until it reaches zero. The final total change in income will be £50m as expected from the formulae used above.

Effect of an initial increase in investment expenditure of £10m

	Change in income (GDP) (£m)	Induced changes in consumption expenditure (£m)
1st round	10	$\frac{4}{5} \times 10 = 8$
2nd round	8	$\frac{4}{5} \times 8 = 6.4$
3rd round	6.4	$\frac{4}{5} \times 6.4 = 5.12$
This process continues		
Total	50	$\frac{4}{5} \times 50 = 40$

PRACTICE QUESTION

1 Given the following information, construct a table showing four rounds of the multiplier.

Initial injection = £12m; MPC = 0.75.

As the only leakage in a two-sector economy is saving, and what is not saved is spent, it follows that

MPS + MPC = 1

This represents a closed economy without a government sector (no taxation) and no spending on imports.

The above equation gives us an alternative way of finding the value of the Keynesian multiplier (K), as shown in the next example.

WORKED EXAMPLE

In a two-sector economy, if MPC = $\frac{4}{5}$, what is the value of the Keynesian multiplier, K?

$$K = \frac{1}{MPS} = \frac{1}{1 - MPC}$$

So $K = \dfrac{1}{1 - \frac{4}{5}} = \dfrac{1}{\frac{1}{5}} = 5$

Or in terms of decimals:

MPC = 0.8

So $K = \dfrac{1}{1 - 0.8} = \dfrac{1}{0.2} = 5$

PRACTICE QUESTION

2 The information in the table shows a two-sector economy where S = I. Saving is given as a percentage of income and the value of the multiplier is given.

Calculate the change in national income.

Income	Percentage consumed	Multiplier
298	75.0	2
349	82.5	1.3
584	63.2	1.7
689	43.5	2.25
721	89.5	0.7

The Keynesian multiplier 2

Four-sector economy

As we saw on pages 72–3, in the case of a two-sector economy the only leakage to be considered was saving, but in a **four-sector economy** we have to consider taxes and imports as well. The proportions of extra income that are spent on taxes and imports are referred to as the **marginal propensity to tax (MPT)** and the **marginal propensity to import (MPM)** respectively. If we refer to the total extra income as 1 again, this gives:

$$1 = \text{MPC} + \text{MPS} + \text{MPT} + \text{MPM}$$

The formulae for these leakages are as follows.

Marginal propensity to consume (the change in consumption due to a change in income):

$$\text{MPC} = \frac{\Delta C}{\Delta Y}$$

Marginal propensity to save (the change in saving due to a change in income):

$$\text{MPS} = \frac{\Delta S}{\Delta Y}$$

Marginal propensity to tax (the change in tax due to a change in income):

$$\text{MPT} = \frac{\Delta T}{\Delta Y}$$

Marginal propensity to import (the change in imports due to a change in income):

$$\text{MPM} = \frac{\Delta M}{\Delta Y}$$

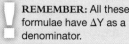

REMEMBER: All these formulae have ΔY as a denominator.

where ΔC = change in consumption; ΔY = change in income; ΔS = change in saving; ΔT = change in tax; and ΔM = change in imports.

If we know the value of the MPC, we can use the same reasoning that we used on page 73 to calculate the value of the multiplier in a four-sector economy, which includes all of the leakages: savings, taxes and imports. This gives the multiplier a value of:

$$K = \frac{1}{\text{MPS} + \text{MPT} + \text{MPM}} = \frac{1}{\text{MPW}}$$

where MPW is the **marginal propensity to withdraw**, which includes all withdrawals.

Since, MPC = 1 – (MPS + MPT + MPM), we can rewrite this expression to obtain:

$$\frac{1}{1 - \text{MPC}} = \frac{1}{\text{MPW}}$$

If MPC is large, then MPW (= 1 – MPC) will be a smaller amount. For example, if MPC is $\frac{9}{10}$ of income, then MPW remaining is $\frac{1}{10}$, giving the multiplier a value of 10; however, if $\frac{1}{2}$ of income is consumed then MPW is $\frac{1}{2}$, giving the multiplier a value of 2. It follows that the larger the MPC the greater the value of the multiplier.

WORKED EXAMPLE

Assume that MPS = 0.1, MPT = 0.25 and MPM = 0.05. Calculate the value of the multiplier, K.

Using the formula:

$$K = \frac{1}{0.1 + 0.25 + 0.05} = \frac{1}{0.4} = 2.5$$

The formula can be used to suit various situations.

WORKED EXAMPLE

Assume that the MPM is 0.1 and the MPS is 0.2, while taxes are equal to 0.25 of income. If the level of national income is £190bn and saving increases by £3bn, calculate the new level of national income.

The MPW = 0.1 + 0.25 + 0.2 = 0.55

So

$$K = \frac{1}{0.55} = 1.82$$

The change in Y = $\Delta Y = K\Delta S$

∴ $\Delta Y = 1.82 \times (-3) = -5.46$

So the new level of income is £190bn − £5.46bn = £184.54bn.

Note that −3 is the figure that represents the increase in taxes and has to be deducted from the national income.

PRACTICE QUESTION

1   Given that income is £200m and the MPS is 0.3, MPT is 0.2 and MPM is 0.1, calculate the effect on the level of national income of an injection of £15m.

STRETCH YOURSELF

Calculate the increase in government spending required to close a negative output gap of £80m where the MPM is 0.18, the MPS is 0.22 and taxes are 20% of income.

Investment 1

The marginal efficiency of capital

According to economic theory a fall in the **rate of interest (ROI)** will lead to an increase in aggregate demand as the components of the formula are all affected by the ROI. This section concentrates on one aspect of aggregate demand: **investment**. The diagram below shows the relationship between investment and the rate of interest when investment in capital equipment increases as the ROI falls. So at R3 the demand for funds to purchase capital is C1, but with a fall in the ROI to R1 the demand for capital increases to C3.

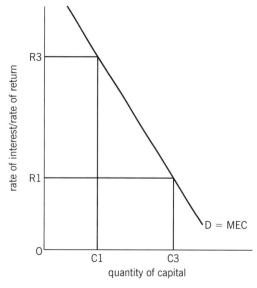

As the curve is downward sloping, capital is subject to the law of diminishing returns. Increasing amounts of capital, if added to a fixed factor, say the quantity of labour or size of the premises, will eventually lead to lower returns.

The **marginal efficiency of capital (MEC)** is the percentage yield or rate of return on capital.

WORKED EXAMPLE

If a machine costs £400,000 and gives a return of £40,000 per year then the MEC, the rate of return on capital, is:

$40,000 \div 400,000 \times 100 = 10\%$ p.a.

Just as the marginal revenue product curve for labour is the firm's demand curve for labour, so the marginal efficiency of capital is the firm's demand for capital. The firm will demand capital if it can make a profit by using it. It will balance the marginal efficiency of capital against the rate of return or yield. Thus if the ROI is higher than the expected yield it will not be profitable for the firm to invest in extra capital.

The table below illustrates a particular firm.

Column 1	Column 2	Column 3	Column 4	Column 5
Number of machines	MPP of capital (units of output)	MRP of capital (£)	Marginal efficiency of capital	
1	75	375	0.375 = 37.5%	
2	70	350	0.350 = 35%	
3	65	325	0.325 = 32.5%	
4	60	300	0.300 = 30%	
5	55	275	0.275 = 27.5%	
6	50	250	0.250 = 25%	

Column 1 shows the number of machines.

Column 2 shows the **marginal physical product (MPP)** of the capital, the amount each machine produces.

Column 3 shows the **marginal revenue product (MRP)** of each machine, assuming that each unit sells for £5, so for one machine (MPP of capital × price = 75 × £5 = £375).

Column 4 shows the marginal efficiency of capital if each machine costs the firm £1,000, where yield/capital = rate of return.

When considering the purchase of capital the firm has to finance it, and whether this is from money that the firm possesses or has to borrow the principle to be considered is balancing cost against yield. With funds that the firm currently possesses the opportunity cost is between buying capital or placing the money with a financial institution to gain interest. If the firm has to borrow, the rate at which it can borrow will be of prime importance.

PRACTICE QUESTION

1 **a** Assuming that each machine is priced as £3,000, with all else remaining the same, calculate the yield per machine and enter it in Column 5.

b How many machines will the firm purchase at a ROI of 10%, and of 6%?

While the MEC is downward sloping and a fall in the ROI will lead to an extension of demand, there are other factors that may lead to a movement of the curve. A shift to the right would show that the MEC of the existing capital stock had increased and also that the firm demands more capital at the existing ROI. Conversely a shift to the left would show that the MEC had fallen and that the firm demands less capital at existing interest rates.

Factors that shift the curve include:

• Business expectations – if entrepreneurs expect future demand to grow they will invest in capital equipment in order to take advantage of it. If their expectations are negative they will not invest.

• A fall in production costs – a fall in the price of capital will increase its yield.

• Increased revenue from output – this will increase the return on capital.

• Reduction in risk – as future returns are uncertain firms include an allowance for risk – if risks are considered to be lower, more capital will be demanded.

• The accelerator effect (see the next section).

Investment 2

The accelerator

The multiplier, as was seen on page 72, describes the relationship between investment and income: how an increase in investment can lead to an increase in employment and income. The **accelerator** looks at how a change in national income can affect investment. We can define it as the relationship between the rate of change of national income and the amount of new induced investment. The theory suggests that the level of planned new investment varies with the rate of change of income or output rather than the rate of interest. A firm is likely to experience a rise in demand for its services as national income increases, and if it is producing close to full capacity it will require extra machines to meet the growing demand for its product. As the cost of the machines is likely to be large when compared with the value of the output, investment expenditure may be extremely large.

 WORKED EXAMPLE

The following example concerns a firm that produces fluorescent tubes and requires £10m of capital equipment to produce £1m of output per year.

Year	Yearly sales (£m)	Stock of capital (£m)	Net (new) investment (£m)
2000	5	50	0
2001	5	50	0
2002	6	60	10
2003	9	90	30
2004	9	90	0
2005	8	80	0
2006	8	80	0

In 2000 and 2001 the firm has sufficient capital to cope with demand, so no new investment takes place.

In 2002 the firm needs £10m of extra capital if it is to fulfil its orders.

In 2003 it has to purchase £30m of extra capital equipment. By the end of 2003 sales have increased by £4m but investment has grown by £40m. This is where the name 'accelerator' comes from, as it shows the effect of a relatively small change in consumption on investment levels.

In 2004 no investment takes place as the firm has 9 machines and can satisfy current demand.

In 2005 and 2006 demand has fallen and the firm has an excess of capital stock and may wish to disinvest by selling some of its used machinery.

The theory suggests that when the growth of national income slows or falls (demand for firms' products slows or falls), new investment will stop, and that in general changes in spending in the economy lead to changes in investment. The effect of this can be large. An increase of 50% in spending between 2002 and 2003 resulted in an increase in investment of 300%.

The value of net investment depends on the magnitude of the accelerator effect. The **capital output ratio** is the ratio of additional capital needed per extra unit of output. It indicates the efficiency of investment. In the example above, £10m of capital was required to produce £1m of goods, giving a capital output ratio of 10. If the ratio falls then capital is becoming more efficient.

The amount of extra capital (ΔK) needed to produce an extra unit of output (ΔQ) is k, the capital output ratio.

$$k = \frac{\Delta K}{\Delta Y}$$

where ΔK is the change in capital, and ΔY is the change in income. The ratio of the amount of capital needed to produce a given quantity of goods to the output.

WORKED EXAMPLE

In terms of the example on page 78 for the years 2001 to 2003:

$\Delta K = \pounds10m + \pounds30m = \pounds40m$

$\Delta Y = \pounds4m$

$k = \Delta K \div \Delta Y = 10$

Thus the total investment (K) in the period is k × the change in income between 2003 and 2001 or

$K = k(Y_n - Y_{n-1})$

$= 10(\pounds90m - \pounds50m) = \pounds40m$

where $Y_n - Y_{n-1}$ is the change in income during the period.

PRACTICE QUESTION

1 Suppose income in Year 1 is £50m and increases by 5% every year for 5 years. Given the formula

$K = k(Y_n - Y_{n-1})$,

calculate the increase in investment during each of the 5 years.

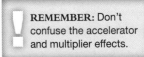

REMEMBER: Don't confuse the accelerator and multiplier effects.

There are some limitations to the theory:

- The model only deals with new investment and ignores replacement investment and about 75% of investment is replacement investment.
- It assumes capital/output ratio is constant over time. New technology can make capital more productive as more advanced machines are likely to be able to produce a greater output. Capital output ratio is likely to be higher in a recession than in a boom. Firms will then not be optimising the use of their capital, but will have excess capacity, and so the capital output ratio will increase.
- The theory suggests that entrepreneurs will react to increased demand by expanding productive capacity. However, this ignores the role of business expectations. These may vary, because entrepreneurs will ask themselves whether a rise in demand is likely to be short-lived, or whether they should take a chance and invest now in order to be ahead of their competitors.

PRACTICE QUESTION

2 The table below considers the relationship between the accelerator, multiplier and effect on the level of national income:

Increased demand (£)	Capital/ output ratio	Net investment required (£)	Multiplier value	Change in national income (£)
50	3	150	2	300
75	2.3	172.5		258.75
196		823.20	3.5	
10	1.9		1.3	
18.2		58.24	1.5	

The first row has been completed for you. The firm's demand increases by £50, and the capital output ratio is 3, so £150 of extra investment is required. The multiplier value is 2, so we would expect the value of the injection to double giving an increase in national income of £300.

a Complete the remainder of the table.

b What are the limitations of the figures that you have calculated?

Absolute and comparative advantage and the terms of trade

Absolute advantage

Suppose there are two countries, A and B:

Country A can produce 100 TVs or 200 tonnes of corn.

Country B can produce 30 TVs or 500 tonnes of corn.

A has an absolute advantage in the production of TVs as it is able to achieve more output than B, which we assume has the same resource input. B has an absolute advantage in the production of corn. The production possibility boundaries of the two countries are shown in the diagram below.

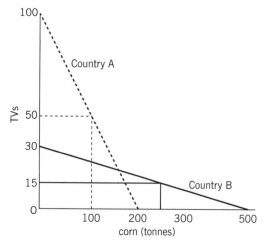 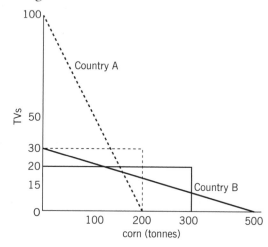

If both countries are self-sufficient and do not trade, and assuming they use half of their resources for each product, then:

A would produce 50 TVs and 100 tonnes of corn – shown in the diagram above left by the broken lines.

B would produce 15 TVs and 250 tonnes of corn – as shown by the solid line in the left-hand diagram.

Total output = 65 TVs and 350 tonnes of corn.

If they both decide to specialise, then A uses its resources for producing 100 TVs and B produces 500 tonnes of corn. Total production has increased from 65 to 100 TVs and from 350 to 500 tonnes of corn.

If the countries decide to trade on the basis of 1 TV to 10 tonnes of corn then A can sell 20 TVs and receive 200 tonnes of corn, increasing its consumption to 80 TVs and 200 tonnes of corn, which is 30 extra TVs and 100 extra tonnes of corn than they would have had without trade.

B can receive 20 TVs and have 300 tonnes of corn, which amounts to an extra 5 TVs and an extra 50 tonnes of corn than they would have had if they had remained self-sufficient.

Trade allows both countries to consume outside their production possibility boundary (PPB) as can be seen in the diagram above right. Both countries have become better off because specialisation according to **absolute advantage** has led to a global reallocation of resources in which production takes place by the most efficient producers.

> **REMEMBER:** These diagrams are for explanation rather than essay use – the conclusion that trade allows consumption beyond the PPB is the major point.

Comparative advantage

In the early 19th century David Ricardo showed that a country could benefit from specialisation and trade even if one country had an absolute advantage in all goods.

Assume that there are two countries, the USA and the UK, and they produce just two commodities, food and clothing, and their output per hour is shown on the following page:

Product	USA		UK	
	Time taken	Units per hour	Time taken	Units per hour
1 unit of food	10 minutes	6	30 minutes	2
1 unit of clothing	20 minutes	3	40 minutes	1.5

Using all of their resources each hour they can produce the output shown in Table 1.

Table 1 Absolute advantage

	USA	UK
Food	6	2
	or	or
Clothing	3	1.5

Table 2 Self-sufficiency

	USA	UK	Total
Food	3	1	4
Clothing	1.5	0.75	2.25

It is clear from Table 1 that the USA has an absolute advantage in the production of both food and clothing as it can produce more than the UK given the same resources.

The USA can produce 1 unit of food in 10 minutes while it takes the UK 30 minutes. The USA is three times as productive as the UK.

With clothing the USA is also more productive and can produce 1 unit of clothing in 20 minutes, while it takes the UK 40 minutes. However, in clothing the USA does not have such comparative superiority: it is only twice as productive in clothing, as opposed to three times as productive in food.

If each country were self-sufficient and used its time equally to produce each product, the output would be as shown in Table 2. Thus, while it would appear at first glance that the USA has little to gain from trade, the theory of comparative advantage argues that resources can be used more efficiently when countries specialise in producing those goods and services in which they have a comparative advantage. **Comparative advantage** means that the **opportunity cost** of producing the good is less in a country than elsewhere, and benefits can be obtained by importing from countries where the opportunity cost is lower and concentrating on exporting something in which a country has a comparative advantage.

✓ WORKED EXAMPLE

Consider the opportunity cost ratios:

In the USA the opportunity cost ratio of food to clothing is $6:3 = 2:1$.

So producing 2 units of food is equivalent to producing 1 unit of clothing.

In the UK the opportunity cost ratio of food to clothing is $2:1.5$. The opportunity cost of food is lower in the USA, so it has a comparative advantage over the UK in the production of food.

In the USA the opportunity cost ratio of clothing to food is $1:2$ (3 clothing to 6 food), whereas in the UK the ratio is $1.5:2$, so more clothing can be produced in the UK for the 2 food. The UK has a comparative advantage in the production of clothing.

Continuing the above example, we can see that with trade both countries can benefit. The benefits to the UK are as follows:

- In the UK one hour's work can produce 1.5 units of clothing or 2 units of food – this is the **domestic rate of exchange**. If the USA trades 6 units of food the UK will exchange $\frac{6}{2} \times 1.5 = 4.5$ units of clothing at their exchange rate of $2:1.5$. Domestically the UK only got 3 units of clothing for 6 units of food, so it has received another 1.5 units of clothing as a result of trade.
- In the UK 1.5 units of clothing exchange for 2 units of food, while in the USA 3 units of clothing exchange for 6 units of food. If the UK trades 1.5 units of clothing with the USA it will receive 3 units of food (at the USA exchange rate of 6 to 3). The UK has received 1 extra unit of food as a result of trade.

Exchange rates

Graphical representation of exchange rates

The exchange rate between two currencies is the price of one in terms of the other.

WORKED EXAMPLE

If the price of a dollar ($) expressed in pounds sterling (£) is 50p, the rate of exchange between pounds sterling and dollars is £1 = $2 making the price of a dollar 50p.

Exchange rates are purely a case of demand and supply, so the rules governing the interaction of both supply and demand are applicable to exchange rates. One difficulty that students encounter is the correct labelling of the *x*- and *y*-axes.

WORKED EXAMPLE

The figure below left shows the demand and supply of dollars on the *x*-axis. The *y*-axis shows the price of dollars in pounds sterling. Whenever you are considering one currency in terms of another, the price of the independent variable is on the *y*-axis while the quantity of the other currency (the dependent variable) is on the *x*-axis.

Demand and supply of dollars

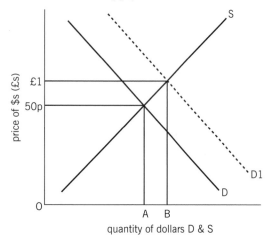

Demand and supply of pounds

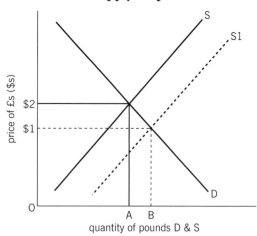

In the diagram on the left the equilibrium price of the dollar is 50p, which means that $1 will exchange for 50p. In terms of export prices it means that $1 spent in the US will purchase 50p worth of UK exports while 50p spent in the UK will buy $1 worth of US imports (ignoring tariffs and transport costs).

REMEMBER: If you are pricing foreign currency in £s the value of the £ is falling as you move up the *y*-axis.

Now assume that the demand for the dollar increases as a result of a rise in income in the UK. The demand curve for dollars shifts from D to D1 and the price of the dollar increases from 50p to £1. (This is the point at which some students become confused – the pound has actually fallen in value compared with the dollar.) Before the increase in the demand for dollars the exchange rate was two dollars to the pound, but now it is only one pound to the dollar. The dollar is now worth more: it has appreciated (increased in value) in relation to the pound while sterling has depreciated (fallen in value), in that it is now worth less in terms of the dollar.

This change has also led to a change in the prices of imports and exports, resulting in a change in the terms of trade. Previously one dollar spent in the US would buy 50p worth of UK exports – now the expenditure of a dollar will buy £1 worth of UK exports as the price of UK goods in the US has fallen.

Previously in the UK, 50p would buy one dollar's worth of US imports; now £1 is required.

When a currency appreciates its exports increase in price while its imports fall in price. The reverse is true for a currency that depreciates: its exports decrease in price while its imports rise in price. Thus, assuming that demand for exports is elastic, for the UK currency depreciation could improve the balance of trade while for the US the appreciation could harm its trading position.

Another area of confusion is that the demand and supply of currencies are a complementary movement. For example, assume that you decide to go on holiday to France; to spend money in France you will require euros. To obtain those euros you may visit a bank, where to obtain the euros you have to offer pounds sterling in exchange. So the demand for one currency has led to the supply of another currency. This can be seen in the right-hand diagram on page 82, which examines the change indicated in the left-hand diagram but from the aspect of the demand and supply of sterling. The initial equilibrium is $2 to the £ (the dollar is worth 50p as shown in the left-hand diagram) indicated by the intersection of the unbroken demand and supply curve. If UK demand for dollars increases (left-hand diagram) there has to be a complementary supply of pounds in exchange (right-hand diagram). Thus the right-hand diagram indicates the original equilibrium where two dollars are exchanged for one pound. The increased supply of sterling, S to S1, leads to a fall in the price of sterling from $2 to $1 as more sterling will only be purchased if the price falls.

PRACTICE QUESTION

1 Assume two currencies – the US$ and the RMB (abbreviation for the Chinese currency). Construct a diagram to show:

   a the effect of a USA balance of payments surplus on the two currencies and

   b the effect of the Chinese selling the RMB.

Formulae for demand and supply

The market for currencies – the foreign exchange market (Forex) – is often portrayed as a near perfect market. A perfect market will clear at the point where $S = D$ and so the equilibrium condition is where $Qd = Qs$, or for market clearing $Qd - Qs = 0$.

The linear demand function is:

$$Qd = a - bP$$

where

Qd = quantity demanded (the dependent variable)
P = price (the independent variable)
a = the quantity intercept
b = the slope $= \dfrac{\Delta Qd}{\Delta P}$. The units of b will depend on the currency used for P.

 WORKED EXAMPLE

Plotting the demand curve for currency from a linear function, $Qd = 50 - 3P$ and by setting P at different values the quantity demanded at each price can be determined.

Start with the Q intercept and assume that $P = 0$.

Then $Qd = 50 - 3 \times 0 = 50$

so we can assume that at zero price 50 will be demanded.

At, say, $P = 10p$, $Qd = 50 - (3 \times 10) = 50 - 30$, so $Qd = 20$.

If the demand curve was to be graphed, then, as the slope is linear, all that would be required would be to join the points for zero price and 10p.

The linear supply function is:

$$Qs = c + dP$$

where

Qs = quantity supplied (the dependent variable)
P = price (the independent variable)
c = the quantity intercept
d = the slope $= \dfrac{\Delta Qs}{\Delta P}$.

Using the formula supply can be calculated in the same way as demand, and the results displayed in tabular form or plotted on a graph.

Using the formula for foreign exchange

In the following example information is provided for both the demand and supply for £s in terms of $s. Using the formula it is possible to calculate the price of £s in $s and the quantity demanded and supplied.

 WORKED EXAMPLE

P represents the price of £s in Chinese RMB, Qd represents the quantity of £s demanded and Qs the quantity of £s supplied.

$Qd = 52 - 3P$
$Qs = 4 + 3P$

Since Qd = Qs at equilibrium,

then $\quad\quad\quad\quad\quad\quad\quad 52 - 3P = 4 + 3P$

Adding 3P to each side, $\quad\quad 52 = 4 + 6P$

Subtracting 4 from each side, $\quad 48 = 6P$

Therefore P = 8 RMB

To determine the volume traded, substitute P = 8 RMB into the equation.

For demand $\quad\quad$ Qd = 52 − 3P

$\quad\quad\quad\quad\quad\quad$ Qd = 52 − 3 × 8

$\quad\quad\quad\quad\quad\quad$ Qd = 52 − 24

Therefore Qd = £28

For supply $\quad\quad$ Qs = 4 + 3P

$\quad\quad\quad\quad\quad\quad$ Qs = 4 + 3 × 8

$\quad\quad\quad\quad\quad\quad$ Qs = 4 + 24

Therefore Qs = £28

PRACTICE QUESTION

1 The following equations show the demand and supply of US dollars in euros.
The letter e denotes the price of the $ in terms of €s. Qd is the quantity of US$ demanded and Qs is the quantity of US$ supplied in millions per week.
Qd = 533.5 − 4e; Qs = 463.2 + 6e
a Calculate the exchange rate of the US$ in €.
b Calculate the amount of US$ traded per week.

Exchange rate conversion

Assume that the exchange rates of one currency ($) in terms of another currency (£) = x. The exchange rate of the second currency (£) in terms of the first ($) is then the reciprocal of x, i.e. $\frac{1}{x}$.

WORKED EXAMPLE

If $1 = £0.50 then £1 = $$\frac{1}{0.50}$ = $2.

PRACTICE QUESTION

2 The table below shows the value of the Albanian lek in terms of other currencies. Calculate the value of these currencies in terms of the Albanian lek and put them in the third column.

Currency	Value of Albanian lek	Currency value in terms of Albanian lek
Algerian dinar	0.7703	
Argentinian peso	0.0640	
Anuba florin	0.0176	
Australian dollar	0.00110	
Bahamian dollar	0.0098	

Purchasing power parity (PPP)

PPP and GDP

Purchasing power parity (PPP) theory is a technique used to compare the purchasing power of different currencies in terms of a common basket of goods. The aim is to prevent the incorrect comparisons that can occur if market exchange rates are used. For example, trying to compare GDP rates or GDP per capita across different countries will produce misleading results because different countries have different price levels. As a result, a unit of money has more purchasing power in a low price country than a high price country. Thus people whose income level means that they are in relative poverty in the UK might have an extremely high standard of living in an impoverished part of the world. As a result, a method of currency conversion is required to account for the different price levels and purchasing power in different countries. This can be seen in the table below, which contains information showing both GDP converted into US$ by means of exchange rates and GDP converted into US$ by means of PPP.

Country	GDP (US$bn) converted by exchange rates (2007)	GDP (US$bn) converted by PPP (2007)
USA	13,751.4	13,751.4
Norway	388.4	251.6
Iceland	20.0	11.1
UK	2772	2143
Bulgaria	39.5	86
Egypt	130.5	403.7
India	1176.9	3096.9

For the bottom three poorest countries GDP figures based on PPPs are higher than those for exchange rates because prices tend to be lower in poorer countries, so GDP appears lower. Excluding the USA, the top three richest countries have lower GDPs when based on PPP. USA figures are identical as the PPP is based on the US$.

Some interesting comparisons are possible. For example, according to GDP based on exchange rates the USA GDP is 11.7 times higher than India's, but when adjusted using PPP the figure falls to 4.4. Clearly assessment of size and living standards cannot be done reliably using GDP based on exchange rates!

PPP and exchange rate adjustment

PPP theory suggests that as market exchange rates tend to fluctuate, trying to compare the GDP of different countries could produce incorrect or misleading results, so PPP using the 'law of one price' argues that, ignoring transport and other transaction costs, market forces will equalise the price of an identical product in two countries.

For example, suppose that the rate of exchange between the UK and France is £1 = €1.50. Then a computer that sells for €375 in France should sell for £250 in the UK. But if the price of the computer was only £218 in the UK, French consumers would prefer to buy their computers in the UK. We would expect that traders wishing to make a profit would purchase computers in the UK and sell them in France and this process would continue until prices had equalised in the two countries.

However, although this is how we expect markets to function, we have to consider that there may be limitations to the operation of the market:

- Transport costs, possible protectionist barriers and other transaction costs like changing euros into sterling may be significant.
- Markets in both countries need to be competitive with no restricted access.
- Some goods and services are not internationally tradable, and will not function in the manner suggested.

Absolute PPP

Absolute PPP refers to the equalisation of price levels across countries. So in the example above the exchange rate between the UK and France is equal to the price level in France divided by the price level in the UK:

$$\text{Exchange rate} = \frac{\text{Price level in France}}{\text{Price level in UK}} = \frac{€375}{£250} = \frac{€1.50}{£1}$$

PPP is an economic theory that estimates the amount of adjustment needed on the exchange rate between countries in order for the exchange to be equivalent to each currency's purchasing power.

The relative version of PPP is calculated as:

$$S = \frac{P1}{P2}$$

where

S represents the exchange rate of currency 1 to currency 2

P1 represents the cost of good x in currency 1

P2 represents the cost of good x in currency 2.

In other words, the exchange rate adjusts so that an identical good in two different countries has the same price when expressed in the same currency. For example, a chocolate bar that sells for CA$1.50 in a Canadian city should cost US$1.00 in a US city when the exchange rate between Canada and the US is 1.50 CAD/USD. (Both chocolate bars cost US$1.00.)

An increase in demand for, say, UK computers would lead to an increase in their price and an increase in the value of the pound sterling relative to the euro. The pound would appreciate and the euro would depreciate.

The table below shows the prices of identical baskets of goods in different countries. Column 1 shows the US price while column 2 shows the price in local currency. Column 3 shows the implied PPP in terms of dollars (column 2 ÷ column 1).

Column 4 shows the actual dollar exchange rate and Column 5 shows the percentage overvaluation or undervaluation of the dollar.

Column 1	Column 2	Column 3	Column 4	Column 5
Price in US ($)	Local price ($)	Implied PPP	Actual $ exchange rate	$ overvaluation/ undervaluation
20	40	2	2.5	+25%
5	15		2.8	
5	1.65		0.4	
7.80	2.87		1.9	
320	343		0.85	
10	13		1.65	

The first calculation has been completed as in the next example.

WORKED EXAMPLE

The actual exchange rate minus the PPP and the result divided by the PPP will result in a figure for overvaluation or undervaluation of the dollar.

$$\text{Overvaluation} = \frac{2.5 - 2}{2} \times 100 = \frac{0.5}{2} \times 100 = 25\%$$

REMEMBER: Carefully check any comparison data to see if it is exchange rate based, PPP based, or HDI based.

The figures are positive, so the dollar is overvalued on the foreign exchange market.

PRACTICE QUESTION

1 Complete the rest of the table above and calculate whether the dollar is overvalued or undervalued.

Relative PPP

Relative purchasing power parity considers the effect of inflation on a country's exchange rate. Inflation reduces the real purchasing power of households. For example, a 5% annual rate of inflation will reduce real income by 5% per year unless workers obtain wage increases.

Relative purchasing power parity examines the relative changes in price levels between two countries and suggests that exchange rates will change to compensate for inflation differentials.

Relative PPP refers to rates of changes of price levels, that is, inflation rates. This proposition states that the rate of appreciation or depreciation of a currency depends on its relative level of inflation compared with other countries. Thus appreciation or depreciation of a currency is equal to the difference in inflation rates between the foreign and the domestic economy.

So, for example if the UK had 5% inflation and Germany had 2% inflation, sterling would depreciate by 3% per year.

This theory is empirically accurate especially if inflation rates are large.

The formula for relative PPP is:

$$\frac{S_1}{S_0} = \frac{1 + I_Y}{1 + I_X}$$

where

S_1 = the exchange rate at the end of the time period

S_0 = the exchange rate at the beginning of the time period – measured as the price of currency Y in terms of currency X

I_Y = the expected inflation rate of a foreign country

I_X = the expected inflation rate in the domestic economy.

The exchange rate used must be the quantity of currency Y (the foreign currency) needed to purchase one unit of currency X (the domestic currency). If we want the initial value of, say, the US dollar in pounds sterling then I_Y must be quoted in pounds per dollar, not dollars per pound.

WORKED EXAMPLE

Assume that the UK's expected rate of inflation is 8% per year while that of France is 2%. It would be expected from what has been said so far that sterling should depreciate by 6% per year and the euro would appreciate by 6% per year relative to the UK.

Assume that the UK is the domestic economy and France is the foreign one.

Current exchange rate is £1 = €1.50.

Expected inflation rates are 2% in the UK and 6% in France.

UK is the domestic currency so $(1 + I_Y) = 1.02$ and $(1 + I_X) = 1.06$

As France has the higher inflation rate we would expect the euro to depreciate

$(I_Y - I_X) = 1.02 - 1.06 = -0.04$ which equals 4%

so the value of the pound would be $(1 - 0.04) \times 1.5 = 0.96 \times 1.5 = 1.44$ euros to the pound.

Alternatively,

$\dfrac{1.02}{1.06} = 0.96226$

$0.96226 \times 1.5 = 1.44$ euros to the pound.

WORKED EXAMPLE

Assume that the UK is the foreign country and China the domestic one.

Current exchange rate is 12RMB to the £. Suppose inflation in the UK is expected to be 5.25% and inflation in China is expected to be 7.5%.

China is the domestic currency so $(1 + I_Y)$ is 1.0525 and $(1 + I_X)$ is 1.075.

As China has the higher inflation it would be expected that the RMB would fall in value by

$(I_Y - I_X) = 1.0525 - 1.075 = -0.0225 = 2.25\%.$

So the expected fall of the RMB to the £ would be $(1 - 0.0225) \times 12 = 11.73$RMB per £.

Or more precisely,

$\dfrac{1.0525}{1.075} \times 12 = 0.979069767 \times 12 = 11.7488$RMB to the pound

---

PRACTICE QUESTION

1 Assume that Morocco is the domestic currency and Spain is the foreign one.

The current exchange rate is 1 Moroccan dirham equals €0.089.

Moroccan inflation is expected to be 19.5% while that of Spain is expected to be 4.45%.

Calculate the likely change in the currency value during the year.

The exchange rate index

Nominal exchange rate

The exchange rate measures the price of one currency in terms of another, e.g. £1 = €1.6. This is the **nominal exchange rate**.

Exchange rates of a currency are an indicator of its international competitiveness. If an exchange rate is falling it may reflect that the country's exports are less competitive. However, as trade is usually with more than one country the difficulty arises that in some cases the value of a currency may be increasing against some trading partners but falling against others. Countries therefore construct an index to indicate the movement of the currency compared with that of their trading partners.

In the UK this is known as the **Sterling Exchange Rate Index (ERI)**.

 WORKED EXAMPLE

The table below shows the value of sterling in terms of the euro, dollar and yen. The numbers in the last column are calculated by subtracting the percentage decrease from 100 or adding the percentage increase to 100. The final figure in the last column is the total of the other three numbers.

Currency	Value of £, year 2000	Base year index 2000	Value of £, year 2001	% increase/ decrease	Index 2001
euro	1.3	100	1.2	−7.6	92.4
dollar	2.0	100	1.75	−12.5	87.5
yen	170	100	180	+6.00	106
					285.9

The indices for 2001 sum to 285.9, so the average index is 285.9 ÷ 3 = 95.3.

This simple index would suggest that overall the value of sterling has fallen against its major trading partners' currencies. However, this will not reflect the true picture as the UK does not do an equal amount of trade with each country. As a result some currency fluctuations are more significant than others. Therefore the index has to be weighted in favour of those trading partners that constitute a larger proportion of a country's exports and imports.

 WORKED EXAMPLE

Suppose that the trading ratios are 50% with the Eurozone, 30% with the USA and 20% with the yen.

Currency	Value of £, year 2000	Base year index 2000	Weighted index	Value of £, year 2001	Index 2001	Index 2001 × weight
euro	1.3	100	500	1.2	92.4	46,200
dollar	2.0	100	300	1.75	87.5	26,250
yen	170	100	200	180	106	21,200
						93,650

The weighted index is 93,650 ÷ 1,000 = 93.65.

The weighted index shows that sterling depreciated further than the simple index suggested, indicating that the competitiveness of UK exports is falling.

PRACTICE QUESTION

1 In 2012 the US$ in terms of Canadian dollars, Mexican pesos and Brazilian reals is worth 1.10, 13.11 and 2.35 respectively, and trade is weighted 45%, 25% and 30% respectively.
Using a table and assuming that the values change in 2013 to 1.45, 14.2 and 2.00 respectively, calculate the trade weighted index.

Real exchange rate

A question that arises is whether the index is only measuring the nominal value of sterling against other currencies or whether it is a **real effective exchange rate index**, where adjustments have been made to take into account inflation and labour costs, and it reflects the true purchasing power of the currency.

For example, assume that it costs the holder of sterling £0.77 to buy €1. From the point of view of the euro holder the nominal exchange rate is £1.30. But as the nominal value does not necessarily indicate the purchasing power of the currency and both parties will want to know what they can buy with the currency that they are purchasing: the real effective exchange rate.

The real effective exchange rate is the nominal effective exchange rate adjusted to take into account both price and labour cost inflation, so it is a better way of comparing economic activity between countries than looking purely at nominal rates. For example, if the value of a currency is falling it could show that other countries are becoming comparatively more productive or have a lower rate of inflation. So comparing real effective exchange rates will show which countries have gained and which have lost international competitiveness.

WORKED EXAMPLE

Suppose that a good which we can call 'X' is sold in two countries. If it sells for £1.30 in the UK and €1 in Europe the prices would equal the exchange rates and the purchasing power parity of the £ and € would be the same.

But suppose that X sells for €1.20 in Europe. That would mean that it costs 20% more in the Eurozone relative to the UK. This would put pressure on the nominal euro rate to adjust as the same good can be purchased more cheaply in one country than another. Thus it would make good sense to buy X in the UK and sell it in the Eurozone! This practice is called **arbitrage** and the people who do it **arbitrageurs**. As they buy £s to buy X to sell in the Eurozone the value of the £ would increase and the value of the euro would fall until real exchange rates return to PPP.

Thus a disconnection between the real and nominal values of the currencies should in a free market lead to a shift in nominal exchange rates until PPP is restored. Undervalued currencies should appreciate and overvalued ones should depreciate. However, in the real world this may happen very slowly or not at all because of government policies like protection and differences in transport costs.

To calculate the real exchange rates the nominal exchange rates are multiplied by the price indices of the two countries: the market price level of goods and services, given by indices of inflation. The equation is:

$$\text{ReR} = \frac{E \times P^{\star}}{P}$$

where

ReR = real exchange rate
E = nominal sterling/euro exchange rate = 1.3
P* = price of X in the Eurozone
P = price of X in the UK.

Terms of trade (TOT)

On pages 80–81 we considered the comparative advantage of trade between the UK and USA. The diagram right shows that the USA will find it advantageous to trade if its terms of trade are 3 units of clothing for every 6 units of food exported. The UK will only trade if it receives 2 units of food for every 1.5 units of clothing exported. In the diagram the terms of trade will lie somewhere between the two possibility boundaries.

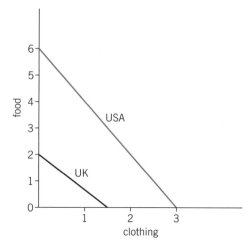

The rate of exchange between food and clothing, or the terms of trade, will determine the benefits of trade for the two trading partners. The **terms of trade (TOT)** are the ratio between export prices and import prices. Movements in the TOT will be caused by inflation, or changes in the value of the currency.

The terms of trade are a concept that relates the prices that a country receives for its exports to the prices it pays for its imports, and can be defined as:

$$\text{Terms of trade (TOT)} = \frac{\text{average price of exports}}{\text{average price of imports}} \times 100$$

If the TOT improve it means that as the price of exports has increased, with the price of imports remaining constant, more imports can be purchased with the same volume of exports. If the TOT improve this is an increase in the value of the ratio of average export prices to average import prices and involves a fall in the opportunity cost of imports. An improvement in the terms of trade can arise from either an increase in the price of exports or a fall in the price of imports.

If the TOT deteriorate it means that less imports can be purchased with the same quantity of exports. A deterioration in the terms of trade represents a decrease in the value of the ratio of average export prices to average import prices and an increase in the opportunity cost of imports. A deterioration can arise from either a fall in the price of exports or an increase in the price of imports.

Measuring and calculating the terms of trade

Export prices and import prices are measured by a weighted price index constructed for each, using a **base year** (see page 90). To calculate the terms of trade, the price index for exports is divided by the price index for imports, and the result is multiplied by 100:

$$\text{Terms of trade} = \frac{\text{index of average export prices}}{\text{index of average import prices}} \times 100$$

WORKED EXAMPLE

Assume that 2011 is the base year where both import and export index = 100.

Suppose that in 2012 the index of export prices is 102 and the index of import prices is 104.

$$\text{Terms of trade in 2012} = \frac{102}{104} \times 100 = 98.08$$

The terms of trade have deteriorated in the period 2011–12: average export prices have fallen relative to average import prices; we can also say that import prices have increased relative to export prices.

Now assume that in 2013 the index of export prices was 112 and the index of import prices was 105. Then

$$\text{terms of trade in 2013} = \frac{112}{105} \times 100 = 106.6$$

The terms of trade have improved and export prices have risen relative to import prices.

Note that a TOT index >1 indicates an improvement in the TOT, whereas a TOT index <1 indicates a deterioration in the TOT.

Effects of changes in the terms of trade (TOT)

Action	Effect on prices	Elasticity	Amount spent	X & M	BOP	Overall effect
1. TOT worsen	Price of exports falls	Elastic	Increases	X increases	↑ Surplus	BOP surplus
	Price of imports rises	Elastic	Decreases	M falls	↓ Deficit	
2. TOT worsen	Price of exports falls	Elastic	Increases	X increases	↑ Surplus	Depends on relative PEODs
	Price of imports rises	Inelastic	Increases	M increases	↑ Deficit	
3. TOT improve	Price of exports rises	Inelastic	Increases	X increases	↑Surplus	BOP surplus
	Price of imports falls	Inelastic	Decreases	M falls	↑ Surplus	
4. TOT improve	Price of exports rises	Elastic	Decreases	X falls	↑Deficit	Depends on relative PEODs
	Price of imports falls	Inelastic	Decreases	M falls	↑Surplus	

In the table both number 1 and number 3 produce a clear effect on the BOP, while numbers 2 and 4 produce indeterminate effects due to the mix of the EODs for demand and supply.

Number 2 represents the position that the UK finds itself in when the TOT move against it:
- As foreign demand for UK exports is elastic, a fall in price will lead to more being spent on UK exports.
- As UK demand for foreign imports is inelastic, a price rise will lead to more being spent on UK imports.
- Thus, if demand for UK exports is more elastic than demand for imports is inelastic, then overall more should be spent on our exports than we spend on foreign imports.

The last of these points expresses the situation adequately and this is a simplified interpretation of the **Marshall–Lerner condition**, which expresses it as:

'When the sum of the elasticities of demand for both exports and imports is greater than one, a fall in the exchange rate (deterioration in the TOT) will lead to an improvement in the current account.'

The Marshall–Lerner condition specifically states that the sum of the elasticities is greater than one, and this would allow the balance of payments to improve if sterling depreciated, even if PEOD for exports was (−)0.75 inelastic as long as PEOD for imports was greater than (−)0.25, as the import and export elasticity when summed would be greater than 1. Thus it is possible for foreign demand to be inelastic because, as in my example, while the amount spent on UK exports would fall, the increased expenditure on imports would be less than the fall in revenue from exports, so the BOP would improve. While the Marshall–Lerner condition looks at the possible effect of devaluation on a current account, any change in the exchange rate will lead to a change in the TOT, and in terms of the BOP the UK gains from deteriorating TOT. However, in terms of short-term benefits, an improving TOT offers the possibility of cheaper imports.

Thus a deterioration in the TOT may be beneficial for UK export sales, but the increased prices of imported goods will add to inflationary pressure – ah well, we can't have it all ways!

PRACTICE QUESTION

1 The UK's terms of trade with the EU have depreciated over the last four years.
   a What would be the effect of this on the UK's current account in terms of overall balance with the EU?
   b How and why might the account with individual countries differ?
   c What is the likely effect on the UK's standard of living?

The balance of payments

The **balance of payments (BOP)** is a record of a country's transactions with the rest of the world over the period of a year. It is divided into the **current account**, the **capital account** and the **financial account**. The three accounts, with the help of a balancing item, sum to zero to indicate where the foreign currency came from in the case of an overspend or what was done with it if receipts exceeded disbursements.

In terms of the current account a major clue to deciding whether a transaction represents an export or import is whether pounds sterling are being changed into foreign currency or foreign currency is being changed into pounds. If UK citizens are changing pounds into foreign currency they are importing, since the money will be spent overseas. If foreign currency is being changed into pounds then it represents an export for the UK.

The current account

The current account comprises four sections: **trade in goods**, **trade in services**, **investment income** and **transfers**. The balance of the trade in goods is often referred to as the **trade balance**.

Summing the four components arrives at the overall current account balance.

WORKED EXAMPLE

The table below shows the figures for the UK for 2012 (sourced from the Office for National Statistics).

Current account for 2012	Exports (X) credits (£m)	Imports (M) debits (£m)	Balance (X − M) (£m)
Trade in goods	299,457	407,350	−107,893
Trade in services	193,353	119,361	73,992
Investment income	161,960	164,234	−2,274
Transfers	17,519	40,574	−23,055
Overall balance			**−59,230**

The numbers in the last column were obtained by subtracting the imports (M) from the exports (X) in each row of the table. The overall balance, obtained by adding the figures in the last column, is negative, i.e. imports exceeded exports by £59,230m in 2012.

In the above example for 2012 the **deficit** − the result of more imports than exports − was £59,230m. This meant that the UK had to find £59,230m in foreign currency to pay for the deficit.

WORKED EXAMPLE

The overall deficit calculated above was 3.2% of the UK's GDP.

To calculate total GDP:

1% of GDP was £59,230m ÷ 3.2 = £18,509.375m

Then UK GDP = £18,509.375m × 100 = £1,850,937.5m = £1,851bn

PRACTICE QUESTION

1

	A 2007 Q2 (£bn)	B 2007 Q3 (£bn)	C 2007 Q4 (£bn)	Q1 2008 (£bn)	Q2 2008 (£bn)	Q3 2008 (£bn)	Q4 2008 (£bn)
Trade in goods	−20.4	−23.8	−24.0	−23.7	−23.4	−23.5	−22.3
Trade in services	10.5	11.2	12.1	?	13.4	12.4	16.2
Investment income	?	3.5	11.2	12.7	7.3	?	0.2
Transfers	−3.1	−3.0	?	−4.0	−3.5	−3.3	−2.9
Current balance	−8.9	?	−5.2	−2.6	−6.1	−7.6	−8.8
% of GDP	−2.5	−3.4	−1.5	−0.7	−1.7	−2.1	?

Use the figures in the table to answer the following.

a Calculate the missing figures.

b Calculate the UK's GDP for A, B and C.

c Using Quarter 1 to 4 for 2008, calculate the annual BOP for that year and the total GDP.

The capital account

The capital account is relatively small compared to the other accounts. It consists of capital transfers and acquisition and disposal of non-produced non-financial assets.

Capital transfers are movements of money but are intended for investment rather than consumption and include money that migrants bring in to or take out of the country and debt forgiveness to highly indebted poor countries.

Acquisition and disposal of non-produced non-financial assets refers to rights to natural resources and the sale of intangible assets, such as patents, copyrights, trademarks, franchises and leases.

WORKED EXAMPLE

The table below shows the figures for the capital account for 2012 for the UK (sourced from the Office for National Statistics).

Capital account for 2012	Credit (£m)	Debit (£m)	Overall balance (£m)
Capital transfers	4,450	1,023	
Non-produced non-financial assets	1,690	1,329	
Total	6,140	2,352	3,788

The overall balance was positive, so the UK was in credit in this part of the account.

The financial account

This account is a sum of the following:
- **Foreign direct investment** is investment by companies setting up plants abroad, e.g. Honda producing cars in Swindon and Dyson producing in Malaysia.
- **Portfolio investment** is investors buying shares, bonds or government debt.
- **Financial derivatives** are a way of trading financial risks, e.g. commodity price risks to firms that may be better suited to manage the risks.
- **Other investments** include short-term flows of money seeking to make a profit – often called 'hot money'.
- **Reserve assets** include holdings of foreign currency and special drawing rights at the International Monetary Fund.

Positive figures in the financial account show inward investment flows, while negative figures show outward investment flows.

WORKED EXAMPLE

Financial account	Net figure (£m)
Direct investment	−8,885
Portfolio investment	+58,444
Derivatives	−430
Other investments	−37
Reserves	+3,121
Total	**+52,213**

The balance of the financial and capital accounts = £3,788m + £52,213m = £56,001m.

The balance of payments is a set of accounts and by tradition accounts must balance.

So   current account = capital account + financial account + the balancing item

Thus   −£59,230m = £56,001m + £3,229m = 0

where the £3,229m is the **balancing item**. The purpose of this is to take into account any errors and omissions and is purely an accounting application to ensure the account balances.

PRACTICE QUESTION

2   The following information is known about the international finances of country X and country Y, both new members of the Eurozone. The figures given are net figures (inflows minus outflows) and have been partially calculated. Calculate any figures missing from the table.

BOP components	Country X (€m)	Country Y (€m)
1. Current account		
Receipts:		
Goods	135,200	?
Services	122,793	159,111
Investment income	84,656	173,128
Transfers	?	16,623
Payments:		
Goods	145,727	309,412
Services	112,434	109,259
Investment income	79,663	141,158
Transfers	28,997	31,388
Current balance	**−11,496**	**−15,506**
2. Capital account		
Transfers	−3,225	2,912
Non-produced/financial	626	307
Capital balance	−2,599	3,219
3. Financial account		
Foreign direct investment	2,301	3,207
Portfolio	5,937	4,861
Derivatives	300	?
Other investment	1,300	8,231
Reserves	?	890
Balance of capital and financial accounts	8,671	16,930
Balancing item	2,825	−1,424